ONLY TRUST HIM

LIFE MESSAGES OF
GREAT CHRISTIANS

Only Trust Him

DWIGHT L. MOODY

Compiled by
JUDITH COUCHMAN

SERVANT PUBLICATIONS
ANN ARBOR, MICHIGAN

Vine Books is an imprint of Servant Publications especially designed to serve
evangelical Christians.

Unless otherwise noted, the Scripture used is from the King James Version of the
Bible. All other verses are from the macBible © 1987, 1988, 1991, 1993 by
Zondervan Corporation. Verses marked NRSV are from the New Revised Standard
Version of the Bible, © 1989 by the Division of Christian Education of the National
Council of Churches of Christ in the United States of America. Used by permission.
All rights reserved. Verses marked NIV have been taken from the HOLY BIBLE,
NEW INTERNATIONAL VERSION © 1973, 1978, 1984 by International Bible
Society. All rights reserved. Macintosh is a trademark of Apple Computer, Inc.

Published by Servant Publications
P.O. Box 8617
Ann Arbor, Michigan 48107

98 99 00 01 10 9 8 7 6 5 4 3 2 1

Printed in the United States of America
ISBN 1-56955-067-0

LIBRARY OF CONGRESS CATALOGING-IN-PUBLICATION DATA

Moody, Dwight Lyman, 1837-1899.
    Only trust Him / Dwight L. Moody ; compiled by Judith Couchman.
        p. cm. — (Life messages of great Christians)
    ISBN 1-56955-067-0 (alk. paper)
    1. Spiritual life—Christianity—Prayer-books and devotions.   2. Devotional calen-
    dars. I. Couchman, Judith, 1953-   . II. Title.   III. Series.
BV4811.M57   1998
242—dc21   98-11340
                                                       CIP

For Charette,
a faithful friend

Contents

Acknowledgments

~

I AM GRATEFUL FOR the editorial team at Servant Publications who worked with me on this devotional: Bert Ghezzi, Liz Heaney, Heidi Hess, and Deena Davis. To be sure, they are competent experts, but I also appreciate them as wonderful friends.

Charette Barta, Opal Couchman, Win Couchman, Madalene Harris, Karen Hilt, Shirley Honeywell, Mae Lammers, and Nancy Lemons also deserve many thanks for their prayers as I worked on this book. May their prayers be multiplied into the lives of its readers.

Introduction

NEVER UNDERESTIMATE THE PERSUASIVENESS of a shoe salesperson.

In 1855, Dwight Lyman Moody came to Christ at age eighteen, after a Sunday school teacher named Edward Kimball found the young man in the stockroom of the Holton shoe store and shared the gospel with him. The next year Moody moved from Boston to Chicago, filled with dreams of making a fortune in the shoe business, and though Moody found success, God had other plans for his sales ability.

While still a salesperson, Moody began teaching Sunday school students in a converted saloon. The classes grew so quickly, friends suggested that Moody start a church, so in his late twenties he founded the Illinois Street Church in Chicago, now called Moody Church. He approached the pastorate with fervor, and the church burgeoned. But after several years God intervened again, placing one of His best salespeople on the road. Moody left the pastorate to become a full-time evangelist, drawing huge crowds to his revivals, and traveling America and Great Britain until his death. He is considered one of the greatest evangelists of all time.

From the prayers and encouragement of his associates, Moody also founded the Chicago Evangelization Society, later renamed Moody Bible Institute. "I'll tell you what I want, and what I have on my heart," explained Moody. "I believe we have to have gap-men to stand between the laity and the ministers; men who are trained to do city mission work. Take men that have the gifts and train them for the work of reaching the people." Moody's vision echoed God's transformation of his life, and "the work of reaching the people" thrives in the school today, affecting lives around the world.[1]

For Moody, trusting God was the only way to live. How could anyone refuse the great love God has for us and the blessings He bestows?

That question frames the content of this devotional, *Only Trust Him,* based on Moody's sermons from his days as an evangelist. The forty selections, slightly edited for contemporary readers, teach us about the glory of the gospel, the way to repentance, a powerful spiritual life, the passionate work of bringing people to God, and our hope of heaven. In addition, each section of the book opens with the lyrics of hymns written by Moody's ministry associate, Ira Sankey.

"Trust Him at all times—not part of the time, but at all times," preached Moody. "If we don't trust Him, of course we don't have peace and joy; but if we trust Him at all times, He never leaves us." Accordingly, Moody proved this with his trusting and trustworthy life.

Judith Couchman,
August, 1997

1. Historical information from the Moody Bible Institute website: http://mbigate.moody.edu:9000/Info/history_inst.htm.

THE GLORY OF THE GOSPEL

Grace! 'tis a charming sound,
Harmonious to the ear;
Heav'n with the echo shall resound,
And all the earth shall hear.
Saved by grace alone!
This is all my plea;
Jesus died for all mankind,
And Jesus died for me.

IRA SANKEY AND PHILIP DODDRIDGE

DWIGHT L. MOODY'S INSIGHT
The glory of the gospel is that Christ came to seek and to save sinners.

DAY 1

The Love of God

Thought for Today

There is no limit to the pursuing love of God.

Wisdom From Scripture

The fierce anger of the Lord will not turn back until he fully accomplishes the purposes of his heart. In days to come you will understand this.

"At that time," declares the Lord, "I will be the God of all the clans of Israel, and they will be my people."

This is what the Lord says: "The people who survive the sword will find favor in the desert; I will come to give rest to Israel."

The Lord appeared to us in the past, saying: "I have loved you with an everlasting love; I have drawn you with loving-kindness.

"I will build you up again and you will be rebuilt, O Virgin Israel. Again you will take up your tambourines and go out to dance with the joyful.

"Again you will plant vineyards on the hills of Samaria; the farmers will plant them and enjoy their fruit.

"There will be a day when watchmen cry out on the hills of Ephraim, 'Come, let us go up to Zion, to the Lord our God.'"

This is what the Lord says: "Sing with joy for Jacob; shout for the foremost of the nations. Make your praises heard, and say, O Lord, save your people, the remnant of Israel."

"See, I will bring them from the land of the north and gather them from the ends of the earth. Among them will be the blind and the lame, expectant mothers and women in labor; a great throng will return.

"They will come with weeping; they will pray as I bring them back. I will lead them beside streams of water on a level path where they will not stumble, because I am Israel's father, and Ephraim is my firstborn son.

"Hear the word of the Lord, O nations; proclaim it in distant coastlands: He who scattered Israel will gather them and will watch over his flock like a shepherd.

"For the Lord will ransom Jacob and redeem them from the hand of those stronger than they.

"They will come and shout for joy on the heights of Zion; they will rejoice in the bounty of the Lord—the grain, the new wine and the oil, the young of the flocks and herds. They will be like a well-watered garden, and they will sorrow no more.

"Then maidens will dance and be glad, young men and old as well. I will turn their mourning into gladness; I will give them comfort and joy instead of sorrow.

"I will satisfy the priests with abundance, and my people will be filled with my bounty," declares the Lord.

JEREMIAH 30:24–31:14, NIV

INSIGHTS FROM DWIGHT L. MOODY

"He hath loved us," says Jeremiah 31:3, "with an everlasting love." Now, there is a difference between human and divine love. The one is fleeting, the other is everlasting. There is no end of God's love.

I can imagine some of you saying, "If God has loved us with an everlasting love, why does the same passage say that

God is angry with the sinner every day?" Why, dear friends, that very word *anger* in the Scriptures is one of the very strongest evidences and expressions of God's love.

Suppose I have two boys, and one of them goes out and lies and swears and steals and gets drunk. If I have no love for him, I don't care what he does; but just because I do love him, it makes me angry to see him take that course. And it is because God loves the sinner that He gets angry with him. That very passage shows how strong God's love is.

Let me tell you, dear friends, God loves you in all your backslidings and wanderings. You may despise His love, and trample it under your feet, and go down to ruin; but it won't be because God doesn't love you.

And that is the way with sinners. You have got to trample the blood of God's Son under your feet if you go down to death—to make light of the blood of the innocent, to make light of the wonderful love of God, to despise it. But whether you do or not, He loves you still.

I can imagine some of you saying, "Why does He not show His love to us?" Why, how can it be any further shown than it is? You say so because you won't read His Word and find out how much He loves you. If you will take a concordance and run through the Scriptures with the word *love*, you will find out how much He loves you; you will find out that it is all one great assurance of His love.

He is continually trying to teach you this one lesson and to win you to Himself by a cross of love. All the burdens He has placed upon the sons of men have been out of pure love, to bring them to Himself. Those who do not believe that God is love are under the power of the Evil One. He has blinded you, and you have been deceived with his lies.

God's dealing has been all with love, love, love—from the

fall of Adam to the present hour. Adam's calamity brought down God's love. No sooner did the news reach heaven than God came down after Adam with His love. That voice that rang through Eden was the voice of love, hunting after the fallen one—"Adam, where art thou?" For all these thousands of years that voice of love has been sounding down the ages. Out of His love He made a way of escape for Adam. God saved him out of His pity and love.

I hear you say, "I do not see, I do not understand how it is that He loves us." What more proof do you want that God loves you? You say, "I am not worthy to be loved." That is true. I will admit that. And He does not love you because you deserve it.

Because you do not deserve it, God offers it to you. You may say, "If I could get rid of my sins, God would love me." But how can you get rid of it until you come to Him? He takes us into His own bosom, and then He cleanses us from sin. He has shed His blood for you. He wants you, and He will redeem you today, if you will let Him.

Dwight L. Moody

Questions to Consider
1. How would you describe the love of God?
2. Are you living in the light of His love?

A Prayerful Response
Lord, thank You for pursuing me with Your everlasting love. Amen.

CHRIST'S BOUNDLESS COMPASSION

THOUGHT FOR TODAY

Christ's compassion for the sinful and hurting knows no bounds.

WISDOM FROM SCRIPTURE

When Jesus landed and saw a large crowd, he had compassion on them and healed their sick.

As evening approached, the disciples came to him and said, "This is a remote place, and it's already getting late. Send the crowds away, so they can go to the villages and buy themselves some food."

Jesus replied, "They do not need to go away. You give them something to eat."

"We have here only five loaves of bread and two fish," they answered.

"Bring them here to me," he said.

And he directed the people to sit down on the grass. Taking the five loaves and the two fish and looking up to heaven, he gave thanks and broke the loaves. Then he gave them to the disciples, and the disciples gave them to the people.

They all ate and were satisfied, and the disciples picked up twelve basketfuls of broken pieces that were left over.

The number of those who ate was about five thousand men, besides women and children.

MATTHEW 14:14-21, NIV

It is often recorded in Scripture that Jesus was moved by compassion. We are told in Matthew 14:13 that after the disciples of John had come to Him and told Him that their master had been beheaded—that he had been put to a cruel death—Jesus went out into a desert place and the multitude followed Him, and when He saw the multitude He had compassion on them and healed their sick.

If He were here tonight, in person, standing in my place, His heart would be moved as He looked down into your faces, because He could also look into your hearts and read the burdens and troubles and sorrow you bear. They are hidden from my eyes, but He knows all about them, and as when the multitude gathered round about Him, He knew how many weary, broken, and aching hearts were there.

But He is here tonight, although we cannot see Him with bodily eyes, and there is not a sorrow, a trouble, or an affliction that any of you are enduring but He knows all about it. He is the same tonight as He was when here upon earth—the same Jesus, the same man of compassion.

When He saw that multitude, He had compassion on it and healed their sick, and I hope He will heal a great many sin-sick souls here, and will bind up a great many broken hearts. There is not a heart so bruised and broken but the Son of God will have compassion upon you, if you will let Him. He came into the world to bring mercy and joy and compassion and love.

Did you ever feel the touch of the hand of Jesus? There is love in it.

There is a story told of a mother who received a dispatch that her boy was mortally wounded. She went to the front, as she knew that those soldiers told to watch these sick and wounded could not watch her boy as she would.

So she went to the doctor and asked, "Would you like me to take care of my boy?"

The doctor said, "We have just let him go to sleep, and if you go to him, the surprise will be so great it might be dangerous to him. He is in a very critical state. I will break the news to him gradually."

"But," said the mother, "he may never wake up. I should so dearly like to see him." Oh, how she longed to see him, and finally the doctor said, "You can see him; but if you wake him up and he dies it will be your fault."

"Well," she said, "I will not wake him up if I may only go by his dying cot and see him." She went to the side of the cot. As she gazed upon him, she could not keep her hand off that pallid forehead, and she laid it gently there. There was love and sympathy in that hand, and the moment the slumbering boy felt it, he said, "Oh, Mother, have you come?"

He knew there was sympathy and affection in the touch of that hand. And if you, oh, sinner, will let Jesus reach out His hand and touch your heart, you, too, will find there is sympathy and love in it.

That every lost soul here may be saved, and come to the arms of our blessed Savior, is the prayer of my heart!

> Jesus, my Savior, to Bethlehem come,
> Born in a manger to sorrow and shame;
> Oh, it was wonderful, blest be His name,
> Seeking for me, seeking for me.
>
> Jesus, my Savior, on Calvary's tree,
> Paid my great debt, and my soul He set free;

Oh, it was wonderful, how could it be!
Dying for me, for me.

Wondrous Love

QUESTIONS TO CONSIDER
1. How do you need Christ's compassion today?
2. What broken places inside you need to be healed by His power?

A PRAYERFUL RESPONSE
Lord, pour Your great compassion into my heart, healing the broken places. Amen.

CHRIST SEEKING SINNERS

THOUGHT FOR TODAY

Even though we aren't seeking Him, Christ searches for us.

WISDOM FROM SCRIPTURE

Jesus entered Jericho and was passing through.

A man was there by the name of Zacchaeus; he was a chief tax collector and was wealthy.

He wanted to see who Jesus was, but being a short man he could not, because of the crowd.

So he ran ahead and climbed a sycamore-fig tree to see him, since Jesus was coming that way.

When Jesus reached the spot, he looked up and said to him, "Zacchaeus, come down immediately. I must stay at your house today."

So he came down at once and welcomed him gladly.

All the people saw this and began to mutter, "He has gone to be the guest of a sinner."

But Zacchaeus stood up and said to the Lord, "Look, Lord! Here and now I give half of my possessions to the poor, and if I have cheated anybody out of anything, I will pay back four times the amount."

Jesus said to him, "Today salvation has come to this house, because this man, too, is a son of Abraham.

"For the Son of Man came to seek and to save what was lost."

LUKE 19:1-10, NIV

"The Son of Man is come to seek and to save that which was lost." To me this is one of the sweetest verses in the whole Bible. In this one short sentence we are told what Christ came into this world for. He came for a purpose; He came to do a work, and in this little verse the whole story is told. He came not to condemn the world but that the world, through Him, might be saved.

A few years ago, the Prince of Wales went to America, and there was great excitement about the Crown Prince coming to our country. The papers took it up and began to discuss it, and a great many were wondering what he came for. Was it to look into the republican government? Was it for his health? Was it to see our institutions? Or for this, or for that? He came and went, but he never told us what he came for.

But when the Prince of heaven came down into this world, He told us what He came for. God sent Him, and He came to do the will of His Father. What was that? "To seek and to save that which was lost." And you cannot find any place in Scripture where a person was ever sent by God to do a work that failed.

God sent Moses to Egypt to bring three million bondsmen up out of the house of bondage into the Promised Land. Did Moses fail? It looked, at first, as if he were going to. If we had been in the court when Pharaoh said to Moses, "Who is God, that we should obey Him?" and ordered him out of his presence, we might have thought it meant failure. But did it? God sent Elijah to stand before Ahab, and it was a bold thing when he told him there should be neither dew nor rain; but did he not lock up the heavens for three years and six months?

Now here is God sending His own beloved Son from His bosom, from the throne, down into this world. Do you think

He is going to fail? Thanks be to God, He can save to the uttermost, and there is not a person in this city who may not find it so, if he or she is willing to be saved.

Last night a man told me he was anxious to be saved, but Christ had never sought for him.

I said, "What are you waiting for?"

"Why," he said, "I am waiting for Christ to call me; as soon as He calls me, I am coming."

Now, I do not believe there is a person in this city that the Spirit of God has not striven with at some period of his life. I do not believe there is a person in this audience but Christ has sought after him. Bear in mind, He takes the place of the seeker. Every person who has ever been saved through these thousands of years was first sought after by God. No sooner did Adam fall than God sought him. He had gone away frightened, and hid himself away among the bushes in the garden, but God took the place of the seeker; and from that day to this God has always had the place of the seeker. No man or woman has been saved but He sought them first.

What do we read in the fifteenth chapter of Luke? There is a shepherd bringing home his sheep into the fold. As they pass in, he stands and numbers them. I can see him counting one, two, three, up to ninety-nine. "But," he says, "I ought to have a hundred. I must have made a mistake," and he counts them over again.

"There are only ninety-nine here; I must have lost one." He does not say, "I will let him find his own way back." No! He takes the place of the seeker; he goes out into the mountain and hunts until he finds the lost one, and then he lays it on his shoulder and brings it home. Undoubtedly, the sheep was very glad to get back to the fold, but it was the shepherd who rejoiced and who called his friends and said, "Rejoice with me."

Then there is that woman who lost the piece of money. Someone perhaps had paid her a bill that day, given her ten pieces of silver. As she retires at night, she takes the money out of her pocket and counts it.

"Why," she says, "I have only nine pieces; I ought to have ten." She counts it over again. Only nine pieces! "Where have I been," she says, "since I got the money? I am sure I have not been out of the house."

She turns her pocket wrong side out, and there she finds a hole in it. Does she wait until the money gets back into her pocket? No. She takes a broom, and lights a candle, and sweeps diligently. She moves the table and the chairs, and all the rest of the furniture, and sweeps in every corner until she finds it. And when she has found it, who rejoices? The piece of money? No, the woman who has found it.

In these parables, Christ brings out the great truth that God takes the place of the seeker. People talk of finding Christ, but it is Christ who first finds them.

Addresses of D.L. Moody

QUESTIONS TO CONSIDER
1. How has Christ been seeking you? How do you know this?
2. What do you think He wants from you?

A PRAYERFUL RESPONSE
Lord, I desire to be sought after and "found" by You. Amen.

DAY 4

WHAT IS CHRIST TO ME?

THOUGHT FOR TODAY

Christ is more than our Savior. He daily delivers us from sin's bondage.

WISDOM FROM SCRIPTURE

"The Lord is my rock, my fortress and my deliverer; my God is my rock, in whom I take refuge, my shield and the horn of my salvation. He is my stronghold, my refuge and my savior.

"In my distress I called to the Lord; I called out to my God. From his temple he heard my voice; my cry came to his ears.

"He reached down from on high and took hold of me; he drew me out of deep waters.

"He rescued me from my powerful enemy, from my foes, who were too strong for me.

"They confronted me in the day of my disaster, but the Lord was my support.

"He brought me out into a spacious place; he rescued me because he delighted in me.

"The Lord has dealt with me according to my righteousness; according to the cleanness of my hands he has rewarded me.

"For I have kept the ways of the Lord; I have not done evil by turning from my God.

"All his laws are before me; I have not turned away from his decrees.

"I have been blameless before him and have kept myself from sin.

"The Lord has rewarded me according to my righteousness, according to my cleanness in his sight.

"To the faithful you show yourself faithful, to the blameless you show yourself blameless, to the pure you show yourself pure, but to the crooked you show yourself shrewd.

"You save the humble, but your eyes are on the haughty to bring them low.

"You are my lamp, O Lord; the Lord turns my darkness into light.

"With your help I can advance against a troop; with my God I can scale a wall."

2 SAMUEL 22:2-3, 7, 17-30, NIV

INSIGHTS FROM DWIGHT L. MOODY

What is Jesus Christ to me? I would like to tell you what He has been to me since I have known Him. And I think if any person here today wants to know Christ, he must first know Him as Savior. "He shall be called Jesus, for He shall save His people from their sins" (Mt 1:21). It is the only name given under heaven—it cannot be said of any other man; it is not said of Moses; it is not said of Elijah; it is not said of any of the prophets or patriarchs or apostles that they could save men—not any other name among men under heaven or in heaven that can save the sinner but the name of Jesus.

And if we are to know Him as our redeemer; and if we are to know Him as our deliverer; and if we are to know Him as our shepherd and our great high priest and our prophet and our king; we must first know Him as our Savior. We must meet Him on the Cross first. We must see Him at Calvary, putting away sin; and when we have seen Him as Savior, then we go on and He unfolds Himself to us, and we see Him in a great many other lights.

He is more than a Savior. After He has saved us, He not only is with us but He delivers us from the power of sin. I don't believe that He comes down here and pardons us and then leaves us in prison. When the children of Israel were put behind the blood down there in Goshen, God said, "When I see the blood, I will pass over you" (Ex 12:13). The blood was their Savior; the blood was their salvation. But then He did something more when He took them out of Goshen, and when He took them out of Egypt, and away from their taskmasters, and out of the land of bondage. Then He was their deliverer.

When they came to the Red Sea, and the mountains were on each side of them, and Pharaoh and his hosts were coming on in the rear, the Red Sea was before them—then they wanted a deliverer. And I venture to say a good many of the children of God have known what it is to come to the Red Sea. You have known what it was to be where you could only look up and cry to God to deliver you. You could not turn to the right; you could not turn to the left; you could not turn back; and the Almighty God came and opened the Red Sea, and you passed over on dry land.

When God delivered them from the hands of the king and from their taskmasters, and brought them out of the house of bondage, and brought them through the Red Sea, He became something else to them; He became their Way.

Now, my friends, listen to what the Son of God says: "I am the way." And if I follow Him, He will not lead me into error; He will not lead me into darkness. He leads out of darkness;

He leads out of bondage. He leads into liberty and into light, and He is the only man who ever trod on this earth whom it is safe to follow in all things. If I follow any person but Jesus Christ, I will get into darkness and bondage. If I follow the "isms" of the day and nothing else, they will lead me into darkness. But if I follow the Son of God, He will lead me into life and light immortal, out of darkness.

As I walked through this hall yesterday morning, I stood and looked up at the wall and saw a Bible text. It says, "I am the way" (Jn 14:6). There is life in these words. "I am the way," says the Son of God. Follow Him and you will be in the right place. And when we are willing to bow our will to God's will and say, "Lord Jesus, I am willing to follow Thee, to receive Thee," then we will be in the right place; there will be no trouble then. We submit our will to God's will, and we submit to God's way and take God's way.

All we have to do is keep our eyes on the Master. Follow Him. He doesn't ask us to go where He has not gone Himself. He doesn't drive you and me, but He says, "Follow me" (Mt 4:19). And if we will become His disciples and follow in His path, we may put our feet in His footprints and follow Him.

Dwight Lyman Moody's Life Work and Gospel Sermons

QUESTIONS TO CONSIDER
1. Do you need to know God as deliverer? If so, in what way?
2. How could you seek God's deliverance from daily sin?

A PRAYERFUL RESPONSE
Lord, deliver me from the bondage of sin and show me Your way. Amen.

CHRIST, THE GOOD SHEPHERD

THOUGHT FOR TODAY

Christ is the Good Shepherd who intimately cares for us, His sheep.

WISDOM FROM SCRIPTURE

[Jesus said,] "I tell you the truth, the man who does not enter the sheep pen by the gate, but climbs in by some other way, is a thief and a robber.

"The man who enters by the gate is the shepherd of his sheep.

"The watchman opens the gate for him, and the sheep listen to his voice. He calls his own sheep by name and leads them out.

"When he has brought out all his own, he goes on ahead of them, and his sheep follow him because they know his voice.

"But they will never follow a stranger; in fact, they will run away from him because they do not recognize a stranger's voice."

Jesus used this figure of speech, but they did not understand what he was telling them.

Therefore Jesus said again, "I tell you the truth, I am the gate for the sheep.

"All who ever came before me were thieves and robbers, but the sheep did not listen to them.

"I am the gate; whoever enters through me will be saved. He will come in and go out, and find pasture.

"The thief comes only to steal and kill and destroy; I

have come that they may have life, and have it to the full.

"I am the good shepherd. The good shepherd lays down his life for the sheep.

"The hired hand is not the shepherd who owns the sheep. So when he sees the wolf coming, he abandons the sheep and runs away. Then the wolf attacks the flock and scatters it.

"The man runs away because he is a hired hand and cares nothing for the sheep.

"I am the good shepherd; I know my sheep and my sheep know me—just as the Father knows me and I know the Father—and I lay down my life for the sheep.

"I have other sheep that are not of this sheep pen. I must bring them also. They too will listen to my voice, and there shall be one flock and one shepherd.

"The reason my Father loves me is that I lay down my life—only to take it up again.

"No one takes it from me, but I lay it down of my own accord. I have authority to lay it down and authority to take it up again. This command I received from my Father."

JOHN 10:1-18, NIV

INSIGHTS FROM DWIGHT L. MOODY

I want to speak about Christ as our keeper. A man who was asked what persuasion he was replied that he was one of the same as the apostle Paul, and he said, "I believe that he is able to keep that which is committed to him" (2 Tm 1:12).

What is this keeping? What does it consist of? If one of you had $100,000 in your pocket and knew that fifteen or twenty thieves had their eyes on you, and wanted to rob you, what would you do? You would find a safe bank and put the money in there and feel safe. Now, every one of you has a precious soul, which the devil is striving to rob you of, and you cannot be safe until you have given it to Christ's keeping. The Lion of the Tribe of Judah is the only One who can safely keep us (see Rv 5:5).

I like to think of Christ as a shepherd. The duty of a shepherd is to take care of his sheep. When a bear attacked David's flock, he seized his spear and slew the intruder, and your Shepherd will take as much care of you.

Oh, what joy in the news to those who can say, "The Lord is my shepherd" (Ps 23:1). Think of the shepherd carefully counting his sheep at the close of the day; one is missing; what does he do? Is he content with his ninety and nine, leaving the missing? No, he safely houses the others and then goes in search of the missing one. Can you not see him hunting for the lost one, going over mountains and rocks and crossing brooks? And what joy there is when the wanderer is found. Oh, what a shepherd is that!

The man who saw a shepherd calling his sheep by name wondered if he could tell one from another, they all looked so much alike. When he inquired on the matter, he was pointed to several little defects on the sheep; one had a black spot, another a torn ear, another a bad toe. One was cross-eyed, and so on. The shepherd knew his sheep by their defects, and I think it is so with the heavenly Father. He knows us all by our defects; and with all our faults He loves us.

I once saw a drove of sheep looking very tired and weary, being hurried on by a shepherd and his dogs; and when they wanted to stop and drink at a brook by the wayside, they were not allowed to but were driven on. I felt that was very unkind of the shepherd; but by and by they stopped before a pair of handsome gates, and the flocks were turned into beautiful green pastures with a clear stream running through them.

Then I knew that I had been hasty. The shepherd had not been unkind, but kind, in not allowing his sheep to drink from that muddy stream in the road; for he had been saving them and taking them on to something better.

So it is with our heavenly Father, our Shepherd. He is compelled to afflict us sometimes while leading us to green pastures. Oh, brethren, let us give thanks that we have such a Good Shepherd to guide and protect us; and though these afflictions may come upon us and seem hard at the time, let us remember His great mercy and loving-kindness, and bow and kiss the rod.

Let us look to God for His blessing.

Great Joy

QUESTIONS TO CONSIDER
1. How do you need the Good Shepherd to protect you?
2. How can you learn to follow Him through the difficult times?

A PRAYERFUL RESPONSE
Lord, lead me through affliction and to Your green pastures. Amen.

DAY 6

THE POWER OF THE BLOOD

THOUGHT FOR TODAY
Christ's blood paid the price for our sins.

WISDOM FROM SCRIPTURE
When Moses had proclaimed every commandment of the law to all the people, he took the blood of calves, together with water, scarlet wool and branches of hyssop, and sprinkled the scroll and all the people.

He said, "This is the blood of the covenant, which God has commanded you to keep."

In the same way, he sprinkled with the blood both the tabernacle and everything used in its ceremonies.

In fact, the law requires that nearly everything be cleansed with blood, and without the shedding of blood there is no forgiveness.

It was necessary, then, for the copies of the heavenly things to be purified with these sacrifices, but the heavenly things themselves with better sacrifices than these.

For Christ did not enter a man-made sanctuary that was only a copy of the true one; he entered heaven itself, now to appear for us in God's presence.

Nor did he enter heaven to offer himself again and again, the way the high priest enters the Most Holy Place every year with blood that is not his own.

Then Christ would have had to suffer many times since the creation of the world. But now he has appeared once for all at the end of the ages to do away with sin by the sacrifice of himself.

Just as man is destined to die once, and after that to face judgment, so Christ was sacrificed once to take away the sins of many people; and he will appear a second time, not to bear sin, but to bring salvation to those who are waiting for him.

HEBREWS 9:19-28, NIV

INSIGHTS FROM DWIGHT L. MOODY

It is said of old Dr. Alexander, of Princeton Seminary, that when he parted with the students who were going to preach the gospel, he would take them by the hand and say, "Young man, make much of the blood—*make much of the blood.*"

As I have traveled up and down Christendom, I have found that a minister who gives a clear sound upon this doctrine is successful. A preacher who covers up the Cross, though he may be an intellectual man, and draw large crowds, cannot touch the heart and conscience. There will be no life there, and his church will be like a gilded sepulcher. Those who preach the doctrine of the Cross, holding up Christ as the sinner's only hope of heaven and as the sinner's only substitute, and make much of the blood, God honors, and souls are always saved where the truth is preached.

I would say, *Make much of the blood.*

May God help us to make much of the blood of His Son. It cost God so much to give us this blood, and shall we try to keep it from the world that is perishing from their need of it? The world can get along without us, but not without Christ. Let us preach Christ in season and out of season. Let us go to the sick and dying and hold up the Savior who came to seek and to save them, and died to redeem them.

It is said of Julian the Apostate in Rome that when he was trying to stamp out Christianity, he was pierced in the side by an arrow. He pulled the arrow out, and taking a handful of blood as it flowed from the wound, threw the arrow into the air, shouting, "Thou Galilean, thou has conquered!" Yes, this Galilean is going to conquer. May God help us to give no uncertain sound on this doctrine.

I would rather give up my life than give up this doctrine. Take that away, and what is my hope of heaven? Am I to depend upon my works? Away with them when it comes to the question of salvation. I must get salvation distinct and separate from works, for it is "to him that worketh not, but believeth on Christ" (Rom 4:5). None will walk the celestial pavement of heaven but those washed in the blood.

The first man that went up to heaven from this earth was probably Abel. You can see Abel putting his little lamb upon the altar, thus placing blood between him and his sin. Abel sang a song the angels could not join in. There must have been one solo song of redemption in heaven, because Abel had no one to join him. But there is a great chorus now, for the redeemed have been going up for thousands of years, and they sing of Him who is worthy to receive honor because He died to save us from condemnation.

An aged minister of the gospel, when dying, said, "Bring me your Bible." Putting his finger on 1 John 1:7, he said, "The blood of Jesus Christ cleanseth us from all sin; I die in hope of this verse."

It wasn't his fifty years of preaching, nor his long life in the Lord's service, but the blood of Christ upon which he relied. When we stand before God's tribunal we shall be pure, even as He is pure, if we are washed in the blood of the Lamb.

During the American war a doctor heard a man saying, "Blood, blood, blood!"

The doctor thought this was because he had seen so much blood shed upon battlefields, and he endeavored to soothe his mind.

The man smiled and said, "I wasn't thinking of the blood upon the battlefield, but I was thinking how precious the blood of Christ is to me as I am dying."

As he died, his lips quivered, "Blood, blood, blood!" and he was gone.

Oh, it will indeed be precious when we come to our dying bed! It will then be worth more to us than all the world! One sin is enough to exclude us from heaven, but one drop of Christ's blood is sufficient to cover all our sins.

Wondrous Love

QUESTIONS TO CONSIDER
1. Do you understand what it means to be washed in Christ's blood? Explain.
2. What does the blood of Jesus mean to you?

A PRAYERFUL RESPONSE
Lord, cleanse my sin with Your redemptive blood. Amen.

DAY 7

Look and Live

Thought for Today

We worship a risen Savior who conquered sin and death.

Wisdom from Scripture

Finally Pilate handed him over to them to be crucified. So the soldiers took charge of Jesus.

Carrying his own cross, he went out to the place of the Skull (which in Aramaic is called Golgotha).

Here they crucified him, and with him two others—one on each side and Jesus in the middle.

Pilate had a notice prepared and fastened to the cross. It read: JESUS OF NAZARETH, THE KING OF THE JEWS.

Many of the Jews read this sign, for the place where Jesus was crucified was near the city, and the sign was written in Aramaic, Latin and Greek.

The chief priests of the Jews protested to Pilate, "Do not write 'The King of the Jews,' but that this man claimed to be king of the Jews."

Pilate answered, "What I have written, I have written."

When the soldiers crucified Jesus, they took his clothes, dividing them into four shares, one for each of them, with the undergarment remaining. This garment was seamless, woven in one piece from top to bottom.

"Let's not tear it," they said to one another. "Let's decide by lot who will get it." This happened that the scripture might be fulfilled which said, "They divided my garments among them and cast lots for my clothing." So this is what the soldiers did.

Near the cross of Jesus stood his mother, his mother's sister, Mary the wife of Clopas, and Mary Magdalene.

When Jesus saw his mother there, and the disciple whom he loved standing nearby, he said to his mother, "Dear woman, here is your son," and to the disciple, "Here is your mother." From that time on, this disciple took her into his home.

Later, knowing that all was now completed, and so that the Scripture would be fulfilled, Jesus said, "I am thirsty."

A jar of wine vinegar was there, so they soaked a sponge in it, put the sponge on a stalk of the hyssop plant, and lifted it to Jesus' lips.

When he had received the drink, Jesus said, "It is finished." With that, he bowed his head and gave up his spirit.

JOHN 19:16-30, NIV

INSIGHTS FROM DWIGHT L. MOODY

When the queen of England sits upon her throne, she has a crown worth millions upon her head. Christ had a crown of thorns put on His head, and a reed was put in His hand, and they put a cast-off robe upon Him; and they pointed the finger of scorn at Him and said, "Hail, King of the Jews!"

Look at Him being led up that hill, His back all bleeding and bare! His disciples have left Him. He is forsaken. Now He treads the path alone. The soldiers guard Him. They take that bleeding body of Jesus and lay Him out upon the Cross. They fasten each hand to the arms of the Cross. A Roman soldier comes up and puts a spike into the hand of the innocent Jesus; that hand that had blessed the people; that hand that had ever been ready to touch the sick and make them whole.

The soldiers drove nails into the palms of His hands and nails into His feet. See Him as with blow after blow the soldiers drive nails into His feet and then take the Cross and put it up, with the Son of God hanging between heaven and earth.

Oh, gaze on that scene! Look into that lovely face; look at the blood trickling down from His side. And will you turn away and say, "I do not care for Him?" Is your heart so hard that you see no beauty in Him? Gaze upon Him and look upon His face. Hark! He speaks. Like the prophets of the old days, He could have called down fire from heaven and consumed them. Does He call down legions of angels to beat back the crowd? No. He says, "Father, forgive them, for they know not what they do!" Hear His piercing cry of love, "Father, forgive them, for they know not what they do!"

Then He said, "I thirst." And they refused Him a draught of water, but they gave Him gall, mixed with vinegar. When He found men athirst down here, He gave them living water.

At last He cries again, "It is finished!" I do not know as there were many on earth who heard it and knew what that meant. It was the shout of the conqueror; it was the shout of victory. Everyone in heaven heard the cry. The angels around the throne heard it; the bells of heaven rang, and it was pealing through heaven, "It is finished!"

The God-man has died, and all sinners have to do is look and live. It is eternal life for a look. Undoubtedly, the dark fiends of hell had been gathered there while that was going on. They thought they were going to triumph then. And those dark waves of death and hell came dashing against Him. He beat them back. See the tide and wind in the great ocean. When the wind is angry, how the great waves come dashing up against the rock, but it stands firm.

So the dark waves of hell seemed to dash up against the

Rock of our salvation, but He beat them back. He was able to take the billows and let them roll over Him. And at last he shouted, "It is finished!" He triumphed over the power of darkness. A glorious triumph it was.

Thanks be to God, we do not worship a dead Savior. He has risen and is coming back again. Oh, lift up your hearts, for the time of your redemption draweth near! He is coming back again. Thank God, that day may come at any moment. Let us be ready. Let us see that we have a glorious hope in Christ, and then let Him come, and we shall be forever with the Lord.

I beg you do not make light of the Lord Jesus Christ, but take Him into your heart and He will be your resurrection and your life. And when your hour shall come to be translated to another world, it will be well with you. If we are in Christ, there will be no darkness or sorrow for us.

The Gospel Awakening

QUESTIONS TO CONSIDER
1. What do Jesus' words, "It is finished," mean to you?
2. How does Christ's work on the cross affect your daily life?

A PRAYERFUL RESPONSE
Lord, thank You for finishing Your work on the cross for me. Amen.

THE GOSPEL OF FREEDOM

THOUGHT FOR TODAY

Jesus sets our spirits free and gives us liberty in Him.

WISDOM FROM SCRIPTURE

Can plunder be taken from warriors, or captives rescued from the fierce?

But this is what the Lord says: "Yes, captives will be taken from warriors, and plunder retrieved from the fierce; I will contend with those who contend with you, and your children I will save.

"I will make your oppressors eat their own flesh; they will be drunk on their own blood, as with wine. Then all mankind will know that I the Lord, am your Savior, your Redeemer, the Mighty One of Jacob."

This is what the Lord says: "Where is your mother's certificate of divorce with which I sent her away? Or to which of my creditors did I sell you? Because of your sins you were sold; because of your transgressions your mother was sent away.

"When I came, why was there no one? When I call, why was there no one to answer? Was my arm too short to ransom you? Do I lack the strength to rescue you? By a mere rebuke I dry up the sea, I turn rivers into a desert; their fish rot for lack of water and die of thirst.

"I clothe the sky with darkness and make sackcloth its covering."

The Sovereign Lord has given me an instructed tongue, to know the word that sustains the weary. He wakens me morning by morning, wakens my ear to listen like one being taught.

The Sovereign Lord has opened my ears, and I have not been rebellious; I have not drawn back.

I offered my back to those who beat me, my cheeks to those who pulled out my beard; I did not hide my face from mocking and spitting.

Because the Sovereign Lord helps me, I will not be disgraced. Therefore have I set my face like flint, and I know I will not be put to shame.

ISAIAH 49:24–50:7, NIV

INSIGHTS FROM DWIGHT L. MOODY

Once the Emperor of Russia had a plan by which he was to liberate the forty million serfs of that country. The Emperor called his council and wanted to have them devise some way to set the slaves at liberty.

After they had conferred about it for six months, one night the councilmen sent in their decision, sealed, that they thought it was not expedient. The Emperor went to the Greek Church that night and partook of the Lord's Supper, and he set his house in order, and the next morning you could hear the tramp of soldiers in the streets of St. Petersburg. The Emperor summoned his guard, and before noon sixty-five thousand men surrounded the palace.

At midnight there came a proclamation that every slave in Russia was forever set free. The proclamation had gone forth, and all the slaves of the realm believed it. They have been free ever since.

Suppose they had not believed it? They never would have gotten the benefit for it. If one man liberated forty million, has not God the power to liberate every captive in your city? If there is a poor slave, if there is a child who wants to be liberated, I have come to show that Christ came to bring liberty to the captive. If you will come to Jesus Christ just as you are, marred as you may be with sin, He will cleanse you of it. He will free you and make you heir to His salvation, if you will only accept it as a gift.

When Wilberforce was trying to get a bill through Parliament to liberate all the slaves under the British flag, away off in the islands, there was great excitement. They were anxious to get their liberty. When they were expecting the vessel which would bring the news that the bill had failed or succeeded, thousands of people went down to the shore to get the first news. The captain of the coming vessel knew how anxious they were to get it. As soon as the vessel was in sight, and he saw the multitude on the shore watching for him, he shouted the words, "Free! Free! Free!" and they took up the cry, and it spread through the island.

Oh, my friends, we proclaim the gospel of freedom with the gospel trumpet, "Free, free!" You will never know what liberty is until you know Christ. This very hour you can be free if you want to be.

If you will believe on the Lord Jesus Christ now, you are free. If you will accept salvation as a gift, it is yours. If you have a bad temper, don't you want to gain the victory over that? Christ will give it to you. Some say they cannot help swearing. Well, let Jesus keep you from it. If you have a strong appetite for liquor, Christ will help you conquer it. He is the deliverer as well as the Savior.

The trouble is, people do not know Christ as a deliverer. They forget that the Son of God came to keep us from sin as well as to forgive it. You may say, "I am afraid I cannot hold out." Christ will hold out for you. There is no mountain He will not climb with you if you will; He will deliver you from your besetting sin. There is no sin in the whole catalog of sins you can name, but Christ will deliver you from it perfectly.

You may have a mean and deceitful heart, as most of us have. Christ can deliver you. We must look to Him and Him alone. Our cry must be only to Him, "Oh, Lord Jesus, deliver me and set me free today." There is a Deliverer today who wants to set you free. He will save you from all your sins. Do you want to be delivered? Do not say no one ever told you the way. He will bring you out of the prison. He will bring you out of bondage. He will put a new song into your mouth if you will let Him. Let us pray that the captive may go free.

Evenings with Moody and Sankey

QUESTIONS TO CONSIDER
1. From what has Christ already set you free?
2. How can you express gratitude to Him?

A PRAYERFUL RESPONSE
Lord, set me free to walk in Your ways, and I will praise You for it. Amen.

PART TWO

THE WAY TO REPENTANCE

I have a Savior, He's pleading in glory,
A dear, loving Savior, tho' earth-friends be few;
And now He is watching in tenderness o'er me,
And oh, that my Savior were your Savior too!

I have a Father: to me He has given
A hope for eternity blessed and true:
And soon He will call me to meet Him in heaven,
But oh, that He'd let me bring you with me too!

IRA SANKEY AND SAMUEL CLUFF

DWIGHT L. MOODY'S INSIGHT
Repentance releases our bondage to sin and ushers us into
friendship with Christ.

DAY 9

THERE IS NO DIFFERENCE

THOUGHT FOR TODAY

In God's eyes, there is no difference among people.

WISDOM FROM SCRIPTURE

What then? Are we any better off? No, not at all; for we have already charged that all, both Jews and Greeks, are under the power of sin, as it is written: "There is no one who is righteous, not even one; there is no one who has understanding, there is no one who seeks God.

"All have turned aside, together they have become worthless; there is no one who shows kindness, there is not even one.

"Their throats are opened graves; they use their tongues to deceive. The venom of vipers is under their lips.

"Their mouths are full of cursing and bitterness.

"Their feet are swift to shed blood; ruin and misery are in their paths, the way of peace they have not known.

"There is no fear of God before their eyes."

Now we know that whatever the law says, it speaks to those who are under the law, so that every mouth may be silenced, and the whole world may be held accountable to God.

For "no human being will be justified in his sight" by deeds prescribed by the law, for through the law comes the knowledge of sin.

But now, apart from law, the righteousness of God has been disclosed, and is attested by the law and the prophets, the righteousness of God through faith in Jesus Christ for all who believe. For there is no distinction, since all have sinned and fall short of the glory of God....

ROMANS 3:10-23, NRSV

INSIGHTS FROM DWIGHT L. MOODY

"There is no distinction." This is one of the hardest truths we have to learn. We are apt to think that we're just a little better than our neighbors, and if we find they are a little better than ourselves, we go to work and try to pull them down to our level.

If you want to find out who and what people are, go to the third chapter of Romans, and there the whole story is told: "There is none righteous, no, not one" (v. 10). "For all have sinned, and come short of the glory of God" (v. 23). All! Some people like to have their lives written before they die. If you would like to read your biography, turn to this chapter and you will find it already written there.

I can imagine someone saying, "I wonder if he really pretends to say there is no difference?" The teetotaler asks, "Am I no better than the drunkard?" Well, I want to say right here it is a good deal better to be temperate than intemperate; a good deal better to be honest than dishonest; it is better for a person to be upright in all transactions than to cheat right and left. But when it comes to the great question of salvation, that does not touch the question at all, because all have sinned and come short of the glory of God.

We are all bad by nature. The old Adam stock was bad, and we cannot bring forth good fruit until we are grafted into the one True Vine. If I have an orchard, and two apple trees in it both bear some bitter apples, perfectly worthless, does it make any difference to say the one tree has perhaps five hundred apples, all bad, and the other only two, all bad? There is no difference. One tree has more fruit than the other, but it is all bad.

So it is with people. One thinks he has only one or two very little sins—God won't notice them—while another person has broken every one of the Ten Commandments! No matter, there is no difference. They are both guilty; they have both broken the Law. The Law demands complete and perfect fulfillment, and if you cannot do that, you are lost, as far as the Law is concerned. "Whosoever shall keep the whole law, and yet offend in one point, he is guilty of all" (Jas 2:10).

Nobody knows what is in the heart but Christ. We are told "the heart is deceitful above all things, and desperately wicked; who can know it?" (Jer 17:9). We do not know our own hearts; none of us have any idea how bad they are. Some bitter things have been written about me, but I know a good many more things about myself that are as bad as any other person. By nature we have hearts in rebellion against God, and we do not even love God unless we are born of the Spirit.

I can understand why people do not like this third chapter of Romans—it is too strong for them. It speaks the truth too plainly. But just because we don't like it, we shall be all the better for having looked at it; very likely we shall find it is exactly what we want, after all. I have noticed that the medicine we do not like is the medicine that will do us good. If we don't think we're as bad as the description, we must take a better look at ourselves.

Thank God, my friends, this is just where the gospel comes in. You ask me what my hope is? It is that Christ died for my sins, in my place, and therefore I can enter into life eternal. You ask the apostle Paul what his hope was? Christ died for our sins. This is the hope in which died all the glorious martyrs of old, in which all who have entered heaven's gate have found their only comfort.

Without Christ, we are all undone. The Law we have broken, and it can only hang over our heads the sharp sword of justice. Even if we could keep the Law from this moment, there remains the unforgiven past.

And you who have never felt the burden of your sin—you who think there is a great deal of difference—you who thank God that you are not as other people—beware! God has nothing to say to the self-righteous. Unless you humble yourself before Him in the dust, and confess before Him your iniquities and sins, the gate of heaven, which is open only for sinners saved by grace, must be shut against you forever!

The Best of D.L. Moody

QUESTIONS TO CONSIDER
1. What is your response to the claim, "there is no difference"?
2. Do you need to confess to God your feelings of superiority toward someone?

A PRAYERFUL RESPONSE
Lord, forgive me for thinking I am better than anyone else. Amen.

Sinners Seeking Christ

Thought for Today

When we seek the Lord with our whole heart, we will find Him.

Wisdom from Scripture

Seek the Lord while he may be found, call upon him while he is near; let the wicked forsake their way, and the unrighteous their thoughts; let them return to the Lord, that he may have mercy on them, and to our God, for he will abundantly pardon.

"For my thoughts are not your thoughts, nor are your ways my ways," says the Lord.

"For as the heavens are higher than the earth, so are my ways higher than your ways and my thoughts than your thoughts.

"For as the rain and the snow come down from heaven, and do not return there until they have watered the earth, making it bring forth and sprout, giving seed to the sower and bread to the eater, so shall my word be that goes out from my mouth; it shall not return to me empty, but it shall accomplish that which I purpose, and succeed in the thing for which I sent it.

"For you shall go out in joy, and be led back in peace; the mountains and the hills before you shall burst into song, and all the trees of the field shall clap their hands.

"Instead of the thorn shall come up the cypress; instead of the brier shall come up the myrtle; and it shall be to the LORD for a memorial, for an everlasting sign that shall not be cut off."

ISAIAH 55:6-13, NRSV

INSIGHTS FROM DWIGHT L. MOODY

When anyone is in earnest about his soul's salvation, he begins to seek God, and it does not take a great while for them to meet. It does not take long for an anxious sinner to meet an eager Savior. What do we read in Jeremiah 29:13? "Ye shall seek me, and find me, when ye shall search for me with all your heart." These are the people who find Christ—those who seek for Him with all their heart.

If we are going to seek for Him and find Him, we must do it with all our hearts. I believe the reason why so few people find Christ is because they do not search for Him with all their hearts; they are not terribly in earnest about their souls salvation. But God is in earnest. Everything God has done proves that He is in earnest about the salvation of people's souls. He has proven it by giving His only Son to die for us. The Son of God was in earnest when He died. And the Lord wants us to be in earnest when it comes to this great question of the soul's salvation.

What we want to see is people really wishing to become Christians, people who are dead earnest about it. When someone says, "Do you want to become a Christian?" the answer is not "Well, I wouldn't mind." My friend, I don't think you will ever get into the kingdom of God until you change your language.

We want people crying from the depth of their hearts, "I want to be saved!" On the Day of Pentecost the cry was, "What shall we do?" These men were in earnest, and they found Christ right there. Three thousand found Him when they sought with all their hearts.

When people see Christ as they do wealth, they will soon find Him. To be sure, the world will raise a cry that they are excited. Let cotton go up 10 or 15 percent before tomorrow morning, and you will see how quickly the merchants get excited. And the papers don't play it down either. They say it is healthy excitement; commerce is getting on. But when you get excited about your soul's salvation and are in earnest, they raise the cry, "Oh, they are getting excited and most unhealthy about these things."

Yet they don't talk about people hastening down to death by the thousands. Hear the piercing cry up to heaven! Yet the church of God slumbers and sleeps. Here and there is an inquirer, and yet they go into the inquiry room as if they were half-asleep. When will people seek for Christ as they seek for wealth, as they seek for honor?

I am told that when the war broke out on the Gold Coast, though it was known that the climate was a very unhealthy one and a great many who went there would never return, hundreds of thousands of men wanted to go. Why? They wanted to get wealth, and from wealth, honor. And if there is a chance of going to India, no end of men are willing to go. To get a little honor they will sacrifice comfort, pleasure, health and everything. What God wants is to have people seeking His kingdom as they seek for honor and wealth.

Will there ever be a better time? Will there ever be a better time for that old man whose locks are growing gray, whose eyes are growing dim and who is hastening to the grave? Is not this the very best time for him? Seek the Lord while He may be found.

To the person in the middle of life, I ask, is this not the best time for you to seek the kingdom of God? Will you ever have a better opportunity? Will Christ ever be more willing to save than now? He says, "Come, for all things are now ready." Not going to be, but are ready now.

To the young person. My friend, is it not the best time for you to seek the kingdom of God? Can you say that you will find Him here tomorrow? You do not know what tomorrow may bring forth.

You may never hear another gospel sermon; you may be hearing the last call. My friend, be wise. Make up your mind that you will seek the kingdom of God now. "Behold now is the accepted time; behold, now is the day of salvation" (2 Cor 6:2).

Christ is inviting you to come. "Come unto Me, all ye that labor and are heavy laden, and I will give you rest" (Mt 11:28).

Oh, may we all find rest in Christ!

Twelve Select Sermons

QUESTIONS TO CONSIDER
1. For you, what does it mean to seek Christ?
2. How do you know if you're seeking Him with your whole heart?

A PRAYERFUL RESPONSE
Lord, I will seek for You with my whole heart. Amen.

DAY 11

Excuses, Excuses

Thought for Today
There is no excuse for refusing God's invitation.

Wisdom From Scripture
He said also to the one who had invited him, "When you give a luncheon or a dinner, do not invite your friends or your brothers or your relatives or rich neighbors, in case they may invite you in return, and you would be repaid.

"But when you give a banquet, invite the poor, the crippled, the lame, and the blind.

"And you will be blessed, because they cannot repay you, for you will be repaid at the resurrection of the righteous."

One of the dinner guests, on hearing this, said to him, "Blessed is anyone who will eat bread in the kingdom of God!"

Then Jesus said to him, "Someone gave a great dinner and invited many.

"At the time for the dinner he sent his slave to say to those who had been invited, 'Come; for everything is ready now.'

"But they all alike began to make excuses. The first said to him, 'I have bought a piece of land, and I must go out and see it; please accept my regrets.'

"Another said, 'I have bought five yoke of oxen, and I am going to try them out; please accept my regrets.'

"Another said, 'I have just been married, and therefore I cannot come.'

"So the slave returned and reported this to his master. Then the owner of the house became angry and said to his slave, 'Go out at once into the streets and lanes of the town and bring in the poor, the crippled, the blind, and the lame.'

"And the slave said, 'Sir, what you ordered has been done, and there is still room.'

"Then the master said to the slave, 'Go out into the roads and lanes, and compel people to come in, so that my house may be filled.'

"For I tell you, none of those who were invited will taste my dinner."

LUKE 14:12-24, NRSV

INSIGHTS FROM DWIGHT L. MOODY

No sooner does anyone begin to preach the gospel than men and women begin to make excuses. It is an old story.

Do you know the origin of excuses? You will find it in Eden. When Adam had sinned, he tried to excuse himself. "The woman whom thou gavest to be with me, she gave me of the tree, and I did eat" (Gen 3:12). He tried to lay the blame on God. Eve tried to lay it on the serpent, and down to the present time, men and women, with one consent, make excuses.

Remember that these men in the parable were not invited to a funeral or to hear some dry lecture or sermon. They were not invited to visit a hospital or a prison or a madhouse to witness some terrible scene or execution—something that would have pained them. They were invited to a feast. The gospel is represented in the Bible as a feast. In the evening of this dispensation there is going to be the Marriage Supper of God's Son. Blessed is he who shall be at the Marriage Supper of the Lamb. If I know my own heart, I would rather have my heart taken from my body this moment, and be present on that glorious day, than have the wealth of the world rolled by my feet and miss that wonderful banquet at the marriage of the Lamb.

Not only was this a feast, but a royal feast. If you had the honor of an invitation from Queen Victoria of England—if the queen invited you to some great banquet in honor of her son, there is not a man or woman who would not accept the invitation. You would want the papers to report how you had been honored. But here is something worth more than that. Here is an invitation from the King of kings, the Lord of lords, God's only Son. By and by He will take his bride into the bridal chamber. The Marriage Supper of the Lamb is hastening on. He has gone to prepare new mansions for His bride. The old mansions are not good enough, and He will come by and by to take her to Himself.

I am inviting you to this feast. The invitations are going out now to every corner of the earth. There is not one here who is not invited. For years God's messengers have been crossing over valley and mountain, over desert and sea, from end to end of the earth, inviting men and women to the gospel feast. What an honor!

When a person prepares a feast, there is a great rush to see who will get the best place. But God prepares His feast, and the chairs would all be empty if His disciples did not go out and compel people to come in.

Then, when people prepare a feast, they invite their friends, those who love them. But God invites His bitterest enemies, those who are in rebellion against Him. And yet we make excuses! No sooner is the invitation given by God than the excuses begin to rain in.

Are you willing to receive the message from God? Do you believe the Word of God is true and that God invites you to this feast? Do you believe that the invitation is to every person in the world? You have nothing to do with the preacher who brings the message. If the message is from God, why not accept it?

If you are going to wait until you find some perfect man or woman to bring you the invitation, you will never accept it. There was never but one perfect Man. You will find a good many flaws in human character, a good many things you may not like in the followers of Christ, but I challenge you to find a flaw in the character of our Master. He bids you come. And anyone who accepts the invitation, He will receive.

Twelve Select Sermons

QUESTIONS TO CONSIDER
1. Do you ever make excuses to God? If so, what are they?
2. Why might you be making these excuses?

A PRAYERFUL RESPONSE
Lord, I will stop making excuses and follow Your way. Amen.

THE PRODIGAL SON

THOUGHT FOR TODAY

God is always ready to take back spiritual prodigals.

WISDOM FROM SCRIPTURE

Then Jesus said, "There was a man who had two sons.

"The younger of them said to his father, 'Father, give me the share of the property that will belong to me.' So he divided his property between them.

"A few days later the younger son gathered all he had and traveled to a distant country, and there he squandered his property in dissolute living.

"When he had spent everything, a severe famine took place throughout that country, and he began to be in need.

"So he went and hired himself out to one of the citizens of that country, who sent him to his fields to feed the pigs.

"He would gladly have filled himself with the pods that the pigs were eating; and no one gave him anything.

"But when he came to himself he said, 'How many of my father's hired hands have bread enough and to spare, but here I am dying of hunger!'

"'I will get up and go to my father, and I will say to him, "Father, I have sinned against heaven and before you; I am no longer worthy to be called your son; treat me like one of your hired hands."'

"So he set off and went to his father. But while he was still far off, his father saw him and was filled with compassion; he ran and put his arms around him and kissed him.

"Then the son said to him, 'Father, I have sinned against

heaven and before you; I am no longer worthy to be called your son.'

"But the father said to his slaves, 'Quickly, bring out a robe—the best one—and put it on him; put a ring on his finger and sandals on his feet.

"'And get the fatted calf and kill it, and let us eat and celebrate; for this son of mine was dead and is alive again; he was lost and is found!' And they began to celebrate."

LUKE 15:11-24, NRSV

INSIGHTS FROM DWIGHT L. MOODY

There was no home for the prodigal among strangers. If the strangers had attempted to give him a home, it would not have been home to him, but they did not. There he was among strangers—coatless, shoeless, hatless. Some of the young men in that country came along, some of the very friends perhaps that had taken his money away from him—for men gambled in those days as they do now—now began to make sport of him.

I can see him straightening himself up and saying to them, "You call me a beggar! Why, my father's servants dress better than you do!"

And they laughed and said, "Your father's servants? Why, you have no father."

No one believed him. He had lost his testimony. And just so has every backslider from God lost his testimony. You can't get any food for the soul in the devil's country. There he was, away from home, starving. Even the food the swine would eat—no one would even give him that. He filled his belly with the husks that the swine ate. Sin had taken him away from Him—away from God—and the point is, how did he get back?

When the man began to come to himself, he woke up to the fact that the best friend he had in the world was his father. There was one thing the prodigal never lost. He lost his work, he lost his food, his home, his testimony, but he never lost his father's love. His father loved him through it all.

I find that a good many people who are living in sin wonder why it is that God does not answer their prayers. Well, God loves them too much to answer their prayers. Suppose the son had written his father a letter, saying, "I am in want, send me some money"? The father would have loved him too well to answer that prayer. Your heavenly Father loves you too well. If you have gone off into a foreign country; if you have gotten away from God's tables, His arms will not reach you there to feed and clothe you. He wants you to come home to Him.

The prodigal had left home and gone into a foreign land, and the famine was upon him. One day a neighbor came down from his native country, perhaps, and found the young man there. Said he, "Why do you not go home?"

"Well, I don't know. I am not sure my father will receive me."

"Your father—he loves you as much as he ever did."

"My father—did you see him?"

"Yes, I was talking with your father one day last week."

"What did he say? Does he ever speak of me?"

"Ever speak of you! He never speaks of anyone else. He dreams of you at night."

Oh, if you are a prodigal, do not go on in that terrible delusion that your father has forgotten you. If a father has nine children, and one is a prodigal away from home, the father thinks more of that one son than he does all the rest.

The whole story of the prodigal is written to demonstrate God's love. It is the only time God is represented as running, just to meet a poor sinner. God walks. When those children of Israel were thrust in that fiery furnace, we find that God walked into that furnace. The story of the prodigal expresses God's love, the compassion of God.

The father of the prodigal did not reproach his boy. He did not have unwelcome words when his son returned from his wanderings. And so God does not reproach the sinner. He knows what human nature is—how liable a mortal is to go astray. It is human to err.

God is always ready to forgive and take you back. Christ says He will forgive. He is full of love and compassion and tenderness. If a sinner comes and confesses, God is willing and ready to forgive him. He will forgive us the hour, yes, the minute, of our return. Oh, you who have gone astray, remember this.

Glad Tidings

QUESTIONS TO CONSIDER
1. In any areas of your life, have you strayed spiritually?
2. If your answer is yes, are you willing to return and accept God's forgiveness?

A PRAYERFUL RESPONSE
Lord, when my heart strays, I want to return to You. Amen.

WHAT IS REPENTANCE?

THOUGHT FOR TODAY
True repentance is choosing to go in a new direction.

WISDOM FROM SCRIPTURE
[Paul said,] "The God who made the world and everything in it, he who is Lord of heaven and earth, does not live in shrines made by human hands, nor is he served by human hands, as though he needed anything, since he himself gives to all mortals life and breath and all things.

"From one ancestor he made all nations to inhabit the whole earth, and he allotted the times of their existence and the boundaries of the places where they would live, so that they would search for God and perhaps grope for him and find him—though indeed he is not far from each one of us.

"For 'In him we live and move and have our being'; as even some of your own poets have said, 'For we too are his offspring.'

"Since we are God's offspring, we ought not to think that the deity is like gold, or silver, or stone, an image formed by the art and imagination of mortals.

"While God has overlooked the times of human ignorance, now he commands all people everywhere to repent, because he has fixed a day on which he will have the world judged in righteousness by a man whom he has appointed, and of this he has given assurance to all by raising him from the dead."

When they heard of the resurrection of the dead, some scoffed; but others said, "We will hear you again about this."

At that point Paul left them.
But some of them joined him and became believers....

ACTS 17:24-34, NRSV

INSIGHTS FROM DWIGHT L. MOODY

The day is appointed. We do not know anything about the calendar of heaven. God has kept that appointment in His own mind. We do not know just the day, but the day is appointed, the time is fixed, and God is going to judge this world. So He sends out a proclamation and commands all people now, everywhere, to repent. And if you do not want to be brought into judgment, you had better turn to God and let Jesus Christ be judged for you, and escape the judgment.

It is a great thing to get rid of the judgment. "There is, therefore, now no condemnation to them who are in Christ Jesus" (Rom 8:1). That is, there is no judgment. Judgment is already past for believers—to the person who has repented of his sins and confessed, and turned away from them, God has put them away. They never again shall be mentioned. We read in Ezekiel that not one of our sins has been mentioned; they have been forgiven. Therefore, God calls upon all people everywhere now—not some future time—but now, to repent.

Repentance is turning right about—as a soldier would call it, "right about-face." As someone has said, people are born with their backs toward God. When someone truly repents, he turns right around and faces God. Repentance is a change of mind. Now, I might feel sorry that I have done a thing, yet go right on and do it over again. But repentance is deeper than feeling. It is action. It is turning right about. God commands all people everywhere to turn.

We need not wait for this kind of feeling, or that kind. It is for us to obey. Do you think God would command us to do something we could not do, and then punish us eternally for not doing it? Do you think God would command all people everywhere to repent and not give them the power to do it? Do you believe it? Away with such an idea as that! He would be an unjust God if He commanded me to do something I could not do and then punished me for not doing it.

Some people say they cannot get an answer to their prayers. If they would get down to the bottom of things, they would find out the reason. They would find there was something not correct in their lives. They haven't made the repentance work deep and thorough. Let us pray for one thing—that the Holy Ghost may convict us all of sins. When will we wake up to the fact that it is more important to live to please God than people?

How sweet our life will be, how pure our conscience will be, if God has forgiven everything, if we have brought everything to light and turned from our sins, and the work has been deep and thorough!

What produces repentance? Paul says in Romans 2:4, "Or despisest thou the riches of his goodness and forbearance and long-suffering; not knowing that the goodness of God leadeth thee to repentance?" Oh, that the Lord may open our eyes and show us how good He has been to us all these years.

The world has a false idea of God. We cannot repent, because we do not turn from that false idea. We have the idea that God hates us—that He is an enemy. That is as false as any lie that ever came out of the pit of hell. There is not any truth in it. God loves the sinner. He so loved the world He gave His only begotten Son to save sinners. Christ died for the ungodly, not the godly; for the sinner, not for the righteous.

God loves you with an everlasting love, although you may

have hated Him and trampled His laws under your feet. He loves you still. May the love of God lead you to repentance.

If you ask for pardon now, He will pardon you. If you want the love of God shed abroad in your heart, turn away from sin and see how quickly He will receive you and how quickly He will bless you.

Moody's Great Sermons

QUESTIONS TO CONSIDER
1. Does your definition of repentance differ from Moody's? Explain.
2. How do you feel about this?

A PRAYERFUL RESPONSE
Lord, I repent of the things in my life that displease You. Amen.

Forgiveness and Retribution

Thought for Today
When we sin, we reap what we sow.

Wisdom From Scripture
So we are always confident; even though we know that while we are at home in the body we are away from the Lord—for we walk by faith, not by sight.

Yes, we do have confidence, and we would rather be away from the body and at home with the Lord.

So whether we are at home or away, we make it our aim to please him.

For all of us must appear before the judgment seat of Christ, so that each may receive recompense for what has been done in the body, whether good or evil.

Therefore, knowing the fear of the Lord, we try to persuade others; but we ourselves are well known to God, and I hope that we are also well known to your consciences.

We are not commending ourselves to you again, but giving you an opportunity to boast about us, so that you may be able to answer those who boast in outward appearance and not in the heart.

For if we are beside ourselves, it is for God; if we are in our right mind, it is for you.

For the love of Christ urges us on, because we are convinced that one has died for all; therefore all have died.

And he died for all, so that those who live might live no longer for themselves, but for him who died and was raised for them.

From now on, therefore, we regard no one from a human point of view; even though we once knew Christ from a human point of view, we know him no longer in that way.

So if anyone is in Christ, there is a new creation: everything old has passed away; see, everything has become new!

All this is from God, who reconciled us to himself through Christ, and has given us the ministry of reconciliation; that is, in Christ God was reconciling the world to himself, not counting their trespasses against them, and entrusting the message of reconciliation to us.

So we are ambassadors for Christ, since God is making his appeal through us; we entreat you on behalf of Christ, be reconciled to God.

2 CORINTHIANS 5:6-20, NRSV

INSIGHTS FROM DWIGHT L. MOODY

I can imagine someone saying, "I attend church and have heard that if we confess our sin, God will forgive us. Now I hear that I must reap the same kind of seed that I have sown. How can I harmonize the doctrine of forgiveness with the doctrine of retribution, and yet you say I must reap what I have sown?"

Suppose I send my hired hand to sow wheat. When it grows up, there are thistles mixed with the wheat. There wasn't a thistle a year ago.

I say to this man, "Do you know anything about the thistles in the field?"

He says, "Yes, I do. You sent me to sow that wheat, and I was angry and mixed thistles with the wheat. But you promised me that if I ever did wrong and confessed it, you would forgive me. Now I hold you to that promise and expect you to forgive me."

"Yes," I say, "you are quite right. I forgive you for sowing the thistles. But I will tell you what you must do—you must reap the thistles along with the wheat when the harvest time comes."

Many Christians are reaping thistles with their wheat. Twenty years ago they sowed thistles with the wheat, and they are reaping them now.

I believe God forgives sin fully and freely for Christ's sake, but He allows certain penalties to remain. If a man has wasted years in riotous living, he can never hope to live them over again. If he has violated his conscience, the scars will remain through life. If he has soiled his reputation, the effect of it can never be washed away.

"John," said a father to his son, "I wish you would get me that hammer."

"Yes, sir."

"Now a nail and a piece of pine board."

"Here they are, sir."

"Will you drive the nail into the board?"

It was done.

"Please pull it out again."

"That's easy, sir."

"Now, John," and the father, his voice dropping to a lower key, "pull out the nail hole."

Every wrong act leaves a scar. Even if the board be a living tree, the scar remains.

It was to Christians that Paul said, "Be not deceived, God is not mocked, for whatever a man soweth, that shall he also reap" (Gal 6:7). God loves us too well not to punish us, His children, when we sin, and He loves us too well to annihilate the secondary consequences of our transgressions. The two sides of the truth must be recognized—that the deep and the primary penalties of our evil, which are separation from God and the painful consciousness of guilt, are swept away. And also that some other results are allowed to remain, but they can be blessed and salutary for the transgressors.

God forgave Moses and Aaron for their sins, but both suffered the penalty. Neither one was permitted to enter the Promised Land. Jacob became a "prince of God" at the ford of Jabbok, but to the end of his days he carried in his body the mark of the struggle. Paul's thorn in the flesh was not removed, even after most earnest and repeated prayer. It lost its sting, however, and became a means of grace.

Perhaps that is one reason why God doesn't remove the evidences of sin. He may intend them to be used as tokens of His chastening. "Whom the Lord loveth he chasteneth" (Heb 12:6). And if the temporary consequence were completely removed, we could be liable to fall back again into sin. The evidence is a continual reminder of our weakness and of the need for caution and dependence upon God.

Sowing and Reaping

QUESTIONS TO CONSIDER
1. Do you carry any scars from past sin? If so, what are they?
2. How can these scars be turned into blessings?

A PRAYERFUL RESPONSE
Lord, I give my scars to You for a work of grace in me. Amen.

How Backsliders May Return

Thought for Today

We can return to God along the same path where we left Him.

Wisdom from Scripture

Go, and proclaim these words toward the north, and say, Return, [backsliding] Israel, says the Lord. I will not look on you in anger, for I am merciful, says the Lord; I will not be angry forever.

Only acknowledge your guilt, that you have rebelled against the Lord your God, and scattered your favors among strangers under every green tree, and have not obeyed my voice, says the Lord.

Return, O faithless children, says the Lord; for I am your master; I will take you, one of a city and two from a family, and I will bring you to Zion. I will give you shepherds after my own heart, who will feed you with knowledge and understanding.

And when you have multiplied and increased in the land, in those days, says the Lord, they shall say no longer say, "The ark of the covenant of the Lord." It shall not come to mind, or be remembered, or missed; nor shall another one be made.

At that time Jerusalem shall be called the throne of the Lord; and all the nations shall gather to it, to the presence of the Lord in Jerusalem, and they shall no longer stubbornly follow their own evil will.

In those days the house of Judah shall join the house of

Israel, and together they shall come from the land of the north to the land that I gave your ancestors for a heritage.

I thought how I would set you among my children, and give you a pleasant land, the most beautiful heritage of all the nations. And I thought you would call me, My Father, and would not turn from following me.

Instead, as a faithless wife leaves her husband, so you have been faithless to me, O house of Israel, says the Lord.

A voice on the bare heights is heard, the plaintive weeping of Israel's children, because they have perverted their way, they have forgotten the Lord their God;

Return, O faithless children, I will heal your faithlessness.

JEREMIAH 3:12-22, NRSV

INSIGHTS FROM DWIGHT L. MOODY

There is one peculiarity about the pit into which the backslider gets: While there are many ways in, there's only one way out. That's the way he got in. The same road that led you away from Christ will take you back.

How did you get away? You all know; everyone who is a backslider knows. You know how you went away. You may say your husband didn't treat you right. Ought not that have driven you nearer to Christ? If you are a man you may say, "My wife hasn't treated me right." Should that have moved you from Christ? Suppose you've got some affliction. God has laid His hand upon you. He does not afflict willingly. Did you ever punish a child? If you did, didn't you do it for the child's good, and not for the pleasure of doing it? I don't see any father and mother who like to do that kind of thing. If they do chasten, it is for the child's good. If you are under the chastening rod of God, don't rebel and think God a hard Master.

Now, if you want to return, there's nothing to hinder you but your own will. Your backslidings can't keep you, because He will blot them all out if you'll let Him. In Jeremiah 3:12, God says, "Go and proclaim these words toward the north, and say, 'Return, thou backsliding Israel ... and I will not cause mine anger to fall upon you.... I will not keep anger forever.'" Do you believe that if Israel had repented, God would have allowed Nebuchadnezzar to take them down to Babylon for seventy years? "Go, proclaim these words and say, 'Return. Only acknowledge thine iniquity, that thou hast transgressed against the Lord, thy God.'"

Of course, if we don't obey the commandments of God, we have backslidden. Everyone who breaks the laws of God is backslidden. You may be in good standing in the church where you belong in the city, in the sight of people, but not in the sight of God. The heart has gotten away, and as long as we are living in rebellion and disloyalty to God and His commandments, we cannot expect the smile of heaven and the blessing of God.

Do you want to come back to God? Commence where you broke off! I will call your attention to another fact. Revelation 2:5 says, "Remember, therefore ... and do the first works, or else I will come unto thee quickly ... except thou repent." Now, people expect that they are going to have the same experience when they repent that they had when they first came to the Lord, but God never repeats Himself. He will give you a fresh experience. But you are to do the first works—repent of your sins; and if there's anything in your life that's wrong, make up your mind that you're going to have that wrong righted, as far as it is in your power. But don't mock God and ask Him to do anything you can do yourself.

It's mockery for me to ask God to do something I can do myself. If I've wronged anyone, and I can make that wrong right, let me go and do it. If a backslider will do that, and do all he can to restore where he has destroyed—consider what his influence for evil has been; how he has led others astray; how he has brought a reproach upon the cause of God in all his backsliding—then he will be in a position to come back and go to work all the harder. I thank God that I've seen many a backslider restored and proved a mighty instrument in God's hands.

God loves you. Come back to the Lord, and He will bless you and use you a thousand times more than He ever did in the past!

"Thou Fool!"

Questions to Consider

1. Have you lost your first love or forgotten to "do the first works"?
2. What might keep you from believing that God will forgive you and use you in His service?

A Prayerful Response

Lord, I will return to You, my first love. Please use me in Your service. Amen.

CHRIST, THE RESTORER

THOUGHT FOR TODAY

Christ not only forgives sin, He restores the soul.

WISDOM FROM SCRIPTURE

Have mercy on me, O God, according to your steadfast love; according to your abundant mercy blot out my transgressions.

Wash me thoroughly from my iniquity, and cleanse me from my sin.

For I know my transgressions, and my sin is ever before me.

Against you, you alone, have I sinned, and done what is evil in your sight, so that you are justified in your sentence and blameless when you pass judgment.

Indeed, I was born guilty, a sinner when my mother conceived me.

You desire truth in the inward being; therefore teach me wisdom in my secret heart.

Purge me with hyssop, and I shall be clean; wash me, and I shall be whiter than snow.

Let me hear joy and gladness; let the bones that you have crushed rejoice.

Hide your face from my sins, and blot out all my iniquities.

Create in me a clean heart, O God, and put a new and right spirit within me.

Do not cast me away from your presence, and do not take your holy spirit from me.

Restore to me the joy of your salvation, and sustain in me a willing spirit.

Then I will teach transgressors your ways, and sinners will return to you.

Deliver me from bloodshed, O God, O God of my salvation, and my tongue will sing aloud of your deliverance.

O Lord, open my lips, and my mouth will declare your praise.

For you have no delight in sacrifice; if I were to give a burnt offering, you would not be pleased.

The sacrifice acceptable to God is a broken spirit; a broken and contrite heart, O God, you will not despise.

Do good to Zion in your good pleasure; rebuild the walls of Jerusalem, then you will delight in right sacrifices, in burnt offerings and whole burnt offerings; then bulls will be offered on your altar.

PSALM 51, NRSV

INSIGHTS FROM DWIGHT L. MOODY

Psalm 23:3 begins, "He restoreth my soul." I love to think of Christ as a restorer. There are many who have strayed away from the fold, who want to come back and be restored to their first love, and this is just what the Lord wants to do for you. If you are full of the joy of the Lord, you will be full of power. Pray today that the Lord will restore your soul.

Pray, as David did, "Restore unto me the joy of thy salvation; and uphold me with a willing spirit. Then will I teach transgressors thy ways, and sinners shall be converted unto thee" (Ps 51:12-13). David got as far away from the Lord as any sinner, but the Lord restored him.

It seems to me that every day I find Christians more troubled about their coldness and distance from God. This psalm is for them. Let them remember that the Lord is able and willing to be a restorer to them.

At the young converts' meeting last night, some were speaking of their trials and battles. The Lord had given them new hearts, but the flesh was rising up to trouble them. Paul tells us what is to be done in such cases: "Likewise, reckon ye also yourselves to be dead indeed unto sin" (Rom 6:11). It doesn't say the old Adam is actually dead. You don't "reckon" people dead if they are dead, and there is no reckoning about it. The thing to do is to treat the old nature as if it were dead—keep it down, keep it under—and God will give you the new nature power to overcome and destroy it.

Another class of person to whom I want to speak a word is those who have once professed to be followers of the Lord Jesus Christ and have left Him and gone back to the world. I want to ask the backslider, "Are you happy?" If you are, you are the first backslider I ever heard of who was happy. I never knew a man or woman who ever found Christ and left Him who had any peace of mind. The world can never fill the void made by the loss of Christ.

Perhaps there was a time when you used to pray, and perhaps now your children ask you, "What has God done that you don't pray to Him anymore?" Why have you left Him? What has Christ done to you that you should leave Him? What Christ wants is to have you come back today.

If you treat Christ as a personal friend, you will never go away from Him. If I were going to leave, I would shake hands with my friends and say, "Good-bye." But did you ever hear of a backslider going into his closet and saying, "Lord, I have served you so long, now I am tired of your service and am going back to the world, so good-bye"? Who ever heard of anyone leaving Christ in that way? You left Him without saying good-bye, but He will have mercy on you if you come back to Him.

May God bring home the wanderers! May they hear the voice of the Shepherd today, in the dark mountains, call them home!

I bring you a loving message. He will forgive you if you will return to Him, even as if you never had wandered. He is the Restorer.

I went to a physician the other day to tell him that a niece of mine, whom he had cured, as we supposed, had suffered a relapse.

"Well," said the doctor, "just increase the remedy."

That is just what the relapsed believer must do—get more of Christ.

Moody: His Words, Work, and Workers

QUESTIONS TO CONSIDER
1. How can you tell if your soul has been restored?
2. How can you "get more of Christ"?

A PRAYERFUL RESPONSE
Lord, please restore my soul, my life, with Your touch. Amen.

PART THREE

THE POWERFUL LIFE

Simply trusting every day,
Trusting through a stormy way;
Even when my faith is small.
Trusting Jesus, that is all.
Trusting as the moments fly,
Trusting as the days go by;
Trusting Him whate'er befall,
Trusting Jesus, that is all.

Brightly doth His spirit shine
Into this poor heart of mine;
While He leads I cannot fall;
Trusting Jesus, that is all.
Trusting as the moments fly,
Trusting as the days go by;
Trusting Him whate'er befall,
Trusting Jesus, that is all.

IRA D. SANKEY AND EDGAR P. STITES

DWIGHT L. MOODY'S INSIGHT
If we trust God at all times, we know He will never forsake us.

Trusting God

Thought for Today

Those who trust God find peace.

Wisdom From Scripture

Open the gates that the righteous nation may enter, the nation that keeps faith.

You will keep in perfect peace him whose mind is steadfast, because he trusts in you.

Trust in the Lord forever, for the Lord, the Lord, is the Rock eternal.

He humbles those who dwell on high, he lays the lofty city low; he levels it to the ground and casts it down to the dust.

Feet trample it down—the feet of the oppressed, the footsteps of the poor.

The path of the righteous is level; O upright One, you make the way of the righteous smooth.

Yes, Lord, walking in the way of your laws, we wait for you; your name and renown are the desire of our hearts.

My soul yearns for you in the night; in the morning my spirit longs for you. When your judgments come upon the earth, the people of the world learn righteousness.

Though grace is shown to the wicked, they do not learn righteousness; even in a land of uprightness they go on doing evil and regard not the majesty of the Lord.

O Lord, your hand is lifted high, but they do not see it. Let them see your zeal for your people and be put to shame; let the fire reserved for your enemies consume them.

Lord, you establish peace for us; all that we have accomplished you have done for us.

ISAIAH 26:2-12, NIV

INSIGHTS FROM DWIGHT L. MOODY

You cannot find anyone who has put his whole trust in God but he has perfect peace. His soul is at rest. This is the reward for those who do.

If we put our trust in our own strength, it will fail us. If we put our trust in our money, some thieves may get it, fires may burn it up, it may take to itself wings. If we put our trust in friends, they will die and leave us. If we trust in anything on earth, we will be disappointed, but if we put our trust in God, He never dies. He never breaks a promise. He is everlasting strength.

All human strength fails. All earthly streams get dry sometimes, but God never fails. The Keeper of Israel never slumbers, never sleeps. Therefore, if our trust is in Him and we look to Him wholly and entirely for everything, we will have peace and joy.

Trust in Him at all times. There are a good many who trust in God when they are not in trouble and don't apparently need to trust, but they do not trust in God when they are in great trouble and difficulty. They do not leave it all with Him and rest assured that everything works together for good to them that love God (see Rom 8:28). This is something they know very little about. Here and there are people willing to trust God when they cannot see how it is coming out.

Trust Him at all times—not part of the time, but at all times. If we don't trust Him, of course we don't have peace and joy, but if we trust Him at all times, the Lord never leaves us. Whoever heard of one being left in a time of trouble when their trust was in God and all their expectations in Him? Trust Him at all times; pour out your heart to Him! God is a refuge for us.

Still I can imagine someone saying, "I don't know what to trust. I have been waiting for that trust. I have been praying for it." I met a woman in the inquiry room the other night who told me she had been praying thirty years for faith that she might trust God. That is not a miraculous trust at all. It is the same kind of trust we have in one another. Don't you know that all business in this city would be suspended if the business people didn't trust one another? Let the business community once lose its confidence, and see how quick business is paralyzed!

You must commit your soul to God and trust Him and rest right there. Certainly when any of you are sick, you trust the doctor. If not, you would not have him come to see you. If you thought he was going to poison you, you would not take his medicine. What you want to do is trust the Great Physician of your soul. Trust Christ; He has never lost a case yet. Trust Him. He will keep you and not let you die. If this great temple we live in dissolves, we have a building death cannot touch, eternal in the heavens, and we save that building just by trust.

If you have a case in court, and don't know anything about the law, you have unbounded confidence in your lawyer, and you leave the case in his hands and trust him to take care of your interests. And so you have a bad case, an awfully bad case, and the best thing you can do now is to commit it to the great Advocate, Jesus Christ. He will take care of your case and bring you out of all your trouble if you only put your trust in Him.

What reason have you for not believing Him? Have you any reason under heaven for not taking God at His word and believing on Him that you might have everlasting life? How is it when you take people at their word? They make promises that often they cannot keep, and which they did not intend to keep when they made them. If you can take people at their word—and you trust them—you can take God at His word. And that is what trust is: taking God at His word.

Hasn't God promised to receive people as they come? If I die, I will die trusting. According to 1 John 5:9–12 "If we receive the witness of men, the witness of God is greater; for this is the witness of God which he hath testified of His Son. He that believeth on the Son of God hath the witness in himself; he that believeth not God hath made him a liar, because he believeth not the record that God gave of His Son. And this is the record, that God hath given to us eternal life, and this life is in His Son. He that hath the Son hath life, and he that hath not the Son of God hath not life."

Fifty Sermons and Evangelistic Talks

QUESTIONS TO CONSIDER
1. Which is more challenging for you: trusting God in peaceful or difficult times? Why?
2. How can you begin to trust God in all things?

A PRAYERFUL RESPONSE
Lord, I will trust You instead of myself and my ideas. Amen.

WALKING WITH GOD

THOUGHT FOR TODAY

God wants to walk with us as a friend.

WISDOM FROM SCRIPTURE

Blessed are they whose ways are blameless, who walk according to the law of the Lord.

Blessed are they who keep his statutes and seek him with all their heart.

They do nothing wrong; they walk in his ways.

You have laid down precepts that are to be fully obeyed.

Oh, that my ways were steadfast in obeying your decrees!

Then I would not be put to shame when I consider all your commands.

I will praise you with an upright heart as I learn your righteous laws.

I will obey your decrees; do not utterly forsake me.

How can a young man keep his way pure? By living according to your word.

I seek you with all my heart; do not let me stray from your commands.

I have hidden your word in my heart that I might not sin against you.

Praise be to you, O Lord; teach me your decrees.

With my lips I recount all the laws that come from your mouth.

I rejoice in following your statutes as one rejoices in great riches.

I meditate on your precepts and consider your ways.

I delight in your decrees; I will not neglect your word.

PSALM 119:1-16, NIV

INSIGHTS FROM DWIGHT L. MOODY

For thousands of years God has been trying to win people back into His company that they might walk with Him. We would be saved from many a dark hour if we were only willing to walk with God, if we would only let Him take us by the hand and lead us through this dark world. He would not lead us into darkness. He would not lead us into trouble and sorrow. He would lead us into the light.

God sent His Son down here to tell us how to walk. In 1 Peter 2:21, it says, "For even hereunto were ye called, because Christ also suffered for us, leaving us as an example, that ye should follow in his steps; Who did no sin, neither was guile found in his mouth; Who, when he was reviled, reviled not again; when he suffered, he threatened not, but committed himself to him that judgeth righteously."

God wants us to follow in His footsteps. I have been told there are some men out on the frontier, in the wilds of America, who in going through the Rocky Mountains will find an Indian trail where there is only one set of footprints, as if only one person had gone over the mountains. I am told by those who know a good deal about those Indians that the chief goes before, and all the rest of the tribe follow him and put their foot into his footsteps.

That is what our Chief wants to do. He has passed through the heavens and gone up on high, and He wants us to follow. Whenever we are tempted, if we would just ask the question, "I wonder if Jesus would do it if He were here?" and be willing to take Him as our guide, what a help that would be!

I am talking now to God's people—to Christians, for no person would have a desire to walk with God until becoming a Christian. You must be subject to the kingdom of God before you will have any desire to follow the King. Leviticus 26:2-4 tells us, "Ye shall keep my Sabbaths, and reverence my sanctuary: I am the Lord. If ye walk in my statutes, and keep my commandments, and do them, then I will give you rain in due season, and the land shall yield her increase, and the trees of the field shall yield their fruit." He tells them how He will bless them and says in verse 12, "And I will walk among you, and will be your God, and ye shall be my people."

If God is walking with us, what power we have! We have nothing to fear, literally nothing, because God, with all His influence, is walking with us. We can walk through into glory; that is what He has promised us we may do. But He gives us a warning in verse 27: "And if ye will not for all this hearken unto me, but walk contrary unto me, then I will walk contrary unto you also in fury; and I, even I, will chastise you seven times for your sins."

What causes all of the trouble in the world? People walking contrary to God. As long as God was walking with Israel, they had power and success, but they did not want Him. They cast Him out; they wanted a king like the nations round about them. What was the result? How quickly they got into trouble, and God had to bring a deliverer to send David. That has been the experience of people for thousands of years. The moment they go away from God and break away from His influence, they get into trouble.

I do not see that we have any better example than Christ Himself. Just consult the Word of God and see what Christ would do. You will find that God never makes a person do wrong. If we are going to keep company with God, we have to walk. God does not stand still nor does He run.

Enoch walked with God. He found the right way back in that dim age. He was the most unpopular man of his time. If he had run for office, I don't think he would have gotten to be as much as a constable. But God and he agreed very well, so that at last God said to him, "Come up here and walk with Me." Old Dr. Bonner said, "Enoch started on a very long walk one way—and he has not gotten back yet."

It is sweet to walk with God. We walk the wilderness today and the Promised Land tomorrow. Oh, that we would all say, "Father, take my hand," and put our hand in His. Abraham walked with God and God became his friend. Let us put our hand in His as a friend, and take hold and walk with Him.

Glad Tidings

Questions to Consider
1. Would you describe your spiritual life as "walking" or "running"? Why?
2. "God does not stand still nor does He run." How do you feel about this statement?

A Prayerful Response
Lord, I will not run ahead of You, but will walk with You this day. Amen.

THE POWER OF GOD

THOUGHT FOR TODAY

Nothing is too hard for God.

WISDOM FROM SCRIPTURE

[Jeremiah prayed,] "Ah, Sovereign Lord, you have made the heavens and the earth by your great power and outstretched arm. Nothing is too hard for you.

"You show love to thousands but bring the punishment for the fathers' sins into the laps of their children after them. O great and powerful God, whose name is the Lord Almighty, great are your purposes and mighty are your deeds. Your eyes are open to all the ways of men; you reward everyone according to his conduct and as his deeds deserve.

"You performed miraculous signs and wonders in Egypt and have continued them to this day, both in Israel and among all mankind, and have gained the renown that is still yours.

"You brought your people Israel out of Egypt with signs and wonders, by a mighty hand and an outstretched arm and with great terror.

"You gave them this land you had sworn to give their forefathers, a land flowing with milk and honey.

"They came in and took possession of it, but they did not obey you or follow your law; they did not do what you commanded them to do. So you brought all this disaster upon them.

"See how the siege ramps are built up to take the city.

Because of the sword, famine and plague, the city will be handed over to the Babylonians who are attacking it. What you said has happened, as you now see.

"And though the city will be handed over to the Babylonians, you, O Sovereign Lord, say to me, 'Buy the field with silver and have the transaction witnessed.'"

Then the word of the Lord came to Jeremiah: "I am the Lord, the God of all mankind. Is anything too hard for me?"

JEREMIAH 32:17-27, NIV

INSIGHTS FROM DWIGHT L. MOODY

God likes His people to believe there is nothing too hard for Him.

We talk about Frederick the Great, Alexander the Great, but how very little are these mighty men when we compare them to God. If Tyndall, or Huxley, or Darwin had ever created any light, what a sound of trumpets would have been about it! But we read in the Bible the very simple statement: "And God said, 'Let there be light': and there was light" (Gn 1:3). And that is all there is said about it.

Here is this earth of ours, 7,920 miles around, with its great oceans and its great mountains and its great rivers, yet it is only a little ball that the Lord tosses out of His hand. The astronomers tell us that the sun is 12,000 times larger than the earth. Besides this, there are millions upon millions of stars. Yet I suppose these are only a few "towns" and "villages" on the outskirts of God's great empire. Now what folly to try to measure God with our little rulers!

I hear somebody saying, "If God is as great as that, He will not condescend to trouble Himself about such an insignificant creature as I."

This is all wrong. If you study the Bible, you will find that no sooner did the news come up to heaven that Adam had fallen than God was right down in Eden after him. Men sometimes get to be so big that they don't care for little things, but God never does. We are constantly limiting God's power by our own ideas. Let us get our eyes off one another and fix them on God. Nothing is too hard for Him.

Whenever I go to a new place, the people say, "Oh, yes, you did so and so in the city, but this place is very peculiar; there are special difficulties here such as you have never met before."

Yes, I suppose there are special difficulties in every case, but those obstacles won't stand in the way very long when God rises up to carry on His work. When Mr. Sankey and I first started out, we took for our motto: "Ah! Lord God, … there is nothing too hard for thee," based on Jeremiah 32:27, and we always had great success. After awhile we thought we would take some other motto, but we couldn't get on at all until we came back to this verse: "Is there anything too hard for thee?"

"And of his fullness have all we received" (Jn 1:16). It is a very common fault with Christians to forget the Lord's fullness. They are living on stale manna and trying to get happy over their past experience. They were converted twenty years ago, and they seem to think the Lord gave them a blessing that was to last them all their lives. Not so. There is an infinite fullness in Christ, and those who believe in Him may receive of it all the time.

Ask Noah. He was able to live and preach 120 years, while he was about the only person in all the world who believed in God, and this he could do because he had received the Lord's fullness. Ask Abraham. He was able to offer up his only son at the command of God. Ask Joshua. He received the fullness, and nobody was able to stand before him all the days of his life.

Now, some people think those old patriarchs and prophets were a different kind of people from us. Not at all. They were people of like passions as us. Yet just let the minister and Christian workers nowadays get filled with the Lord's fullness, and they will be like giants filled with new wine.

There were the reformers Knox, Wesley, Whitefield, and Newton. Were they any greater men in intellect than a great many others in their time? By no means, but they received the Lord's fullness. That was what made them so great and strong in their work. Take the twelve apostles; they were not men of learning and science, they were not great orators, they were not rich, they had no special position. But just think of a Galilean fisherman writing such a book as the Gospel of John! He had received the Lord's fullness.

Moody: His Words, Work, and Workers

QUESTIONS TO CONSIDER
1. What do you think Moody meant by receiving "the Lord's fullness"?
2. How might you accept more of God's power in your life?

A PRAYERFUL RESPONSE
Lord, I want to walk in the fullness of Your power. Amen.

DAY 20

The Christian's Warfare

Thought for Today

Believing in Christ's promises, we can overcome the world.

Wisdom From Scripture

This is love for God: to obey his commands. And his commands are not burdensome, for everyone born of God overcomes the world. This is the victory that has overcome the world, even our faith.

Who is it that overcomes the world? Only he who believes that Jesus is the Son of God.

This is the one who came by water and blood—Jesus Christ. He did not come by water only, but by water and blood. And it is the Spirit who testifies, because the Spirit is the truth.

For there are three that testify: the Spirit, the water, and the blood; and the three are in agreement.

We accept man's testimony, but God's testimony is greater because it is the testimony of God, which he has given about his Son.

Anyone who believes in the Son of God has this testimony in his heart. Anyone who does not believe God has made him out to be a liar, because he has not believed the testimony God has given about his Son.

And this is the testimony: God has given us eternal life, and this life is in his Son.

He who has the Son has life; he who does not have the Son of God does not have life.

I write these things to you who believe in the name of

the Son of God so that you may know that you have eternal life.

This is the confidence we have in approaching God: that if we ask anything according to his will, he hears us.

And if we know that he hears us—whatever we ask—we know that we have what we asked of him.

1 JOHN 5:3-15, NIV

INSIGHTS FROM DWIGHT L. MOODY

When a battle is fought, all are anxious to know who are the victors. In these verses, we are told who gains the victory in life.

When I was converted, I made this mistake: I thought the battle was already won, the crown already in my grasp. I thought that old things had passed away, that all things had become new; that my old corrupt nature, the Adam life, was gone. But I found out, after serving Christ for a few months, that conversion was only like enlisting in the army, that there was a battle on hand, and that if I was to get a crown I had to work for it and fight for it.

Salvation is a gift, as free as the air we breathe. We obtain it like any other gift, without money and without price; there are no other terms. On the other hand, if we are to gain a crown, we must work for it. Let me quote a few verses in 1 Corinthians 3: "For other foundation can no man lay than that which is laid, which is Jesus Christ. Now if any man build upon this foundation gold, silver, precious stones, wood, hay, stubble—every man's work shall be made manifest; for the day shall declare it, because it shall be revealed by fire; and the fire shall try every man's work of what sort it is. If any man's work abide which he hath built thereupon, he shall receive a reward. If any man's work shall be burned, he shall suffer loss;

but he himself shall be saved, yet so as by fire" (vv. 11-15).

We see clearly from this that we may be saved even if all our works are burned up. I may have a wretched, miserable voyage through life, with no victory and no reward at the end; saved yet by fire, or as Job puts it, "with the skin of my teeth." I believe that a great many people will barely get to heaven as Lot got out of Sodom, burned out, nothing left, works and everything else destroyed.

It is like this: When a man enters the army, he is a member of the army the moment he enlists; he is just as much a member as a man who has been in the army ten or twenty years. But enlisting is one thing and participating in a battle another.

It is folly for any person to attempt to fight with his own strength. The world, the flesh, and the devil are too much for any person. But if we are linked to Christ by faith, and He has formed in us the hope of glory, then we shall get the victory over every enemy. Believers are the overcomers. Through Him we shall be more than conquerors.

I wouldn't think of talking to unconverted people about overcoming the world, for it is utterly impossible. They might as well try to cut down the American forest with their penknives. But a good many Christian people make this mistake: They think the battle is already fought and won. They have an idea that all they have to do is to put out the oars, and the current will drift them into the ocean of God's eternal love. But we have to cross the current. We have to learn how to watch and fight and how to overcome. The battle is only just commenced. The Christian life is a conflict and a warfare, and the quicker we find it out, the better.

There isn't a blessing in this world that God hasn't likened Himself to. All the great and higher blessings God associates with Himself. When God and people work together, then there is going to be victory. We are co-workers with Him.

You might take a mill and put it forty feet above a river, and there isn't enough capital in the United States to make that river turn the mill. But let it down about forty feet, and away it works. We want to keep in mind that if we are going to overcome the world, we have to work with God. It is His power that makes all the means of grace effectual.

The story is told that Frederick Douglas, the great slave orator, once said in a mournful speech, when things looked dark for his race: "The white man is against us, governments are against us, the spirit of the times is against us. I see no hope for the colored race. I am full of sadness."

Just then a woman rose in the audience and said, "Frederick, is God dead?"

My friend, it makes a difference when you count God in.

The Overcoming Life

QUESTIONS TO CONSIDER
1. What does being a spiritual overcomer mean to you?
2. Do you consider yourself an overcomer?

A PRAYERFUL RESPONSE
Lord, with You as my strength, I choose to overcome the world's influence on me. Amen.

THE HOLY SPIRIT AND HIS WORK

THOUGHT FOR TODAY
The Holy Spirit gives us love, hope, and liberty.

WISDOM FROM SCRIPTURE
Therefore, since we have been justified through faith, we have peace with God through our Lord Jesus Christ, through whom we have gained access by faith into this grace in which we now stand. And we rejoice in the hope of the glory of God.

Not only so, but we also rejoice in our sufferings, because we know that suffering produces perseverance; perseverance, character; and character, hope.

And hope does not disappoint us, because God has poured out his love into our hearts by the Holy Spirit, whom he has given us.

You see, at just the right time, when we were still powerless, Christ died for the ungodly.

Very rarely will anyone die for a righteous man, though for a good man someone might possibly dare to die.

But God demonstrates his own love for us in this: While we were still sinners, Christ died for us.

Since we have now been justified by his blood, how much more shall we be saved from God's wrath through him!

For if, when we were God's enemies, we were reconciled to him through the death of his Son, how much more, having been reconciled, shall we be saved through his life!

Not only is this so, but we also rejoice in God through

our Lord Jesus Christ, through whom we have now received reconciliation.

ROMANS 5:1-11, NIV

INSIGHTS FROM DWIGHT L. MOODY

There is not a better evangelist in the world than the Holy Spirit. If the churches would just let Him come in, there would soon be a mighty work for Christ.

You may say that what the Church wants today more than anything else is love. In Galatians 5:22-23, we find what should dwell in the churches. There are nine qualities or fruits of the Holy Spirit—peace, gentleness, long-suffering, faith, patience, charity, goodness, joy, self-control—but you can sum them all into one—love.

I read something bearing on this subject: "The fruit of the Spirit is one word—love. Joy is love exalted. Peace is love in repose. Long-suffering is love enduring. Gentleness is love in society. Goodness is love in action. Faith is love on the battle-field. Meekness is love in school. Temperance is love in training."

When the fruit of the Spirit is in my heart, I can love those who hate me. To love a person who thinks a great deal of you is natural love, but to love those who hate you is a different thing, and whenever a person gets the Spirit, he loves his enemies. The Spirit of Christ comes to our souls. When they reviled Him, He cried, "Father, forgive them; for they know not what they do" (Lk 23:34).

I can tell if a church has love. When it isn't there, when the sermon is over, the people rise up and walk out. They don't speak to each other. They do just as if they were at the theater or a concert. But if the love of God is there, the people gather in little groups and talk about how much good the sermon did them, and they will carry it home to their families and tell it to their neighbors. My friends, the great want of the present day in American churches is the want of the love of God in the heart of their members, shed by the Holy Spirit. We cannot love Him, we cannot serve Him, till we have His love in our hearts.

The Holy Spirit also imparts hope. In Romans 15:13, we find, "Now the God of hope will fill you with all joy and peace in believing, that ye may abound in hope through the power of the Holy Spirit." Just let the Spirit begin to work in the churches, and see how powerful they become. The ministry is lifted up, the people are lifted up—all are rejoicing. Take a minister who has lost hope in his church, and as soon as he gets discouraged there's no power there. The Spirit not only imparts love, He gives hope.

I never saw a Christian that had much of the Holy Spirit who got discouraged. I have yet to find a Christian with the Spirit who is not hopeful. Why, they are mounting up on wings of hope, higher, higher, all the time, just like a man who had two bags of gas on either side of him. Whenever he touched the ground he would leap over a hill, over trees, over fences. So when we're full of hope, we rise up.

The Holy Spirit is here now. He is just knocking at the door of every church, and it will be sharp and thorough and lasting if you let Him in. Let Him into your heart, and let Him fill you with His influence.

The Spirit also gives us liberty. See what Paul says in 2 Corinthians 3:17, "Now the Lord is that Spirit; and where the Sprit of the Lord is, there is liberty." What do the workers want any more than liberty? What do the workers require more than liberty?

It is easy to preach when we have the Spirit of God with us. We're not afraid of public opinion at all—we have perfect liberty. The meeting last Monday night in Farwell Hall was one of the best I ever attended. Why? Because we had perfect liberty there. The Spirit of the Lord was there. The rich and poor, the educated and uneducated, high and low assembled and were all free. I don't know of anything that retards the growth of the cause of Christ in churches more than the stiffness, the coldness, in them. There's no liberty when there's stiffness.

When we have the Spirit, we are not afraid of the opinion of our neighbor, of the opinion of this person or that person. We say, "What can I do for the Son of God?" When Christians have the Spirit, they're as free as air. Christ came for that. He didn't come to set us free and then leave us in servitude. He came to give us liberty now and forever.

New Sermons, Addresses, and Prayers of Dwight Lyman Moody

QUESTIONS TO CONSIDER
1. If you live by the Spirit's love and hope, how does it affect your life?
2. What does it mean to you to walk in the Spirit's liberty?

A PRAYERFUL RESPONSE
Lord, show me how to live in the love, hope, and liberty of Your Spirit. Amen.

TRUE PRAYER

THOUGHT FOR TODAY

God wants to abundantly answer our prayers.

WISDOM FROM SCRIPTURE

[Jesus said,] "Ask and it will be given to you; seek and you will find; knock and the door will be opened to you.

"For everyone who asks receives; he who seeks finds; and to him who knocks, the door will be opened.

"Which of you, if his son asks for bread, will give him a stone?

"Or if he asks for a fish, will give him a snake?

"If you, then, though you are evil, know how to give good gifts to your children, how much more will your Father in heaven give good gifts to those who ask him!

"So in everything, do to others what you would have them do to you, for this sums up the Law and the Prophets.

"Enter through the narrow gate. For wide is the gate and broad is the road that leads to destruction, and many enter through it.

"But small is the gate and narrow the road that leads to life, and only a few find it."

MATTHEW 7:7-20, NIV

INSIGHTS FROM DWIGHT L. MOODY

I have no sympathy with the idea that if we ask God to do a certain work, He is going to give us chaff. If we have faith to claim, I believe God will answer our prayers. I don't believe He mocks His children. I believe He will give out of His

103

abundance and give us the very best He has.

Now, I have no doubt that a great many of you have said at different times, "What is the use of prayer, anyway?" Sometimes, when I have prayed, it has seemed as if the heavens were closed over me. It seems as if God does not hear. My words all seem to come back to me. Have you ever felt that way?

In answer to that, let me say in the first place that Jesus Christ is an example for us. We profess to be His disciples. Remember that as a man, He prayed. As God, He answers prayer. The key to Christ's character and life is that He was God-man. At times, He spoke as God; at times, He spoke as man. At times, He acted as a man; at times, as God. But there is one thing you will find. His life, all through His ministry, was filled with prayer, and there was no great event in His life that was not preceded by prayer. All through His public ministry, you will find Him often in prayer.

If you and I are going to hear from heaven, it will be when we are praying. I have often said that I would rather be able to pray like Daniel than preach like Gabriel. What we want is men and women who know how to pray, who know how to call down fire from heaven. Do you have the power with God in prayer? Some of you think you cannot do much in this work, and you have said, "I wish I were stronger. I wish I were not so confined to my household duties." But I want to say that you may accomplish just as much if you cannot come out to any of the meetings. It may be that the bedridden saint in this city will do more toward bringing down fire than all the pastors put together.

I went to London in 1872, just to spend three or four months, and one night I spoke in a prayer meeting. I went into a Congregational church, and I preached with no unusual power. There didn't seem to be anything out of the regular line in the service. In fact, I was a little disappointed. I didn't seem to have much liberty there.

That evening, I preached to a group of men. There seemed to be great power, as if the building was filled with the glory of God, and I asked for an expression of faith when I finished. People rose by the hundreds.

I said, "They don't know what this means," so I thought I would put them to another test. I asked them to step back into the chapel. All those who wanted to become Christians, but no one else. They flocked into the chapel by the hundreds. I was in great perplexity. I couldn't understand what it meant.

I went to Dublin the next day, and on Tuesday morning, I got a dispatch saying, *Come to London at once and help us.*

I didn't know what to make of it, but I hastened back to London and labored there ten days, and there were four hundred names recorded at that time. For months I couldn't understand what it meant, but by and by I found out. There was a poor bedridden woman, and she had taken different ones upon her heart, and she began to pray to God to revive the whole church. She began to pray to send me to that church.

On Sunday morning her sister came home and said, "Who do you think preached for us this morning?"

She guessed a number of ministers who had been in the habit of exchanging with the pastor, and finally gave up.

The sister said, "Mr. Moody, from America."

The woman turned pale and said, "I know what this means; it is an answer to prayer. There is going to be a great work here."

The servants brought up her dinner, but she said, "No. No dinner for me today. I spend this day in prayer." And that night while I was preaching, she was praying, and in answer to her prayer the power of God fell upon the audience.

My dear friends, I believe that when God's books are opened, there will be some hidden people who will be much nearer the throne than you and I.

Dwight Lyman Moody's Life Work and Gospel Sermons

QUESTIONS TO CONSIDER
1. What prayer do you need answered from God's abundance?
2. What more do you want to learn about prayer?

A PRAYERFUL RESPONSE
Lord, teach me both the hiddenness and abundance of prayer. Amen.

THE POWER OF FAITH

THOUGHT FOR TODAY

Our faith can profoundly change other people's lives.

WISDOM FROM SCRIPTURE

A few days later, when Jesus again entered Capernaum, the people heard that he had come home.

So many gathered that there was no room left, not even outside the door, and he preached the word to them.

Some men came, bringing to him a paralytic, carried by four of them.

Since they could not get him to Jesus because of the crowd, they made an opening in the roof above Jesus and, after digging through it, lowered the mat the paralyzed man was lying on.

When Jesus saw their faith, he said to the paralytic, "Son, your sins are forgiven."

Now some teachers of the law were sitting there, thinking to themselves, "Why does this fellow talk like that? He's blaspheming! Who can forgive sins but God alone?"

Immediately Jesus knew in his spirit that this was what they were thinking in their hearts, and he said to them, "Why are you thinking these things?

"Which is easier: to say to the paralytic, 'Your sins are forgiven,' or to say, 'Get up, take your mat and walk?'

"But that you may know that the Son of Man has authority on earth to forgive sins...." He said to the paralytic, "I tell you, get up, take your mat and go home."

He got up, took his mat and walked out in full view of

them all. This amazed everyone and they praised God, saying, "We have never seen anything like this!"

MARK 2:1-12, NIV

INSIGHTS FROM DWIGHT L. MOODY

There are many people who say, "Oh, we can reason out all the miracles of Christ," and they tell us there's nothing of the supernatural that cannot be explained. Everything is in accordance with scientific laws.

These doctors of the law who had come down from Jerusalem and Galilee and Judea attempted this, but had to admit, "We have seen strange things today." They had seen a man who was stricken with palsy, at a word from Christ, walk down the street. I would like to have seen him arrive home and observe his wife and children looking with amazement at him, and hear the children clap their hands for joy as he lay down his bed, saying, "Here wife, I've used that bed a good while. It's carried me long enough. I don't need it any longer."

The Son of Man had cleansed him, and not only that, He had forgiven his sins. The four men had taken him to Christ to get rid of his palsy, and he had gotten rid of all his sins besides.

The thought I want to call to your attention is this: The faith of those four men did the whole thing. Remember this. Skeptics need to remember, too, that if we have faith, God can win them through our faith. The Lord can bless through our faith even those who have no faith.

I remember one of the meetings at Nashville, during the war, when a young man came to me, trembling from head to foot. "What is the trouble?" I asked.

"I got this letter from my sister, and she tells me that every night as the sun goes down, she gets on her knees and prays for me." This man was brave and had been in a number of battles. He could stand before the cannon's mouth, yet this letter completely upset him.

"I have been trembling ever since I received it," he said.

Six hundred miles away, the faith of this woman went to work, and its influence was felt by her brother. He did not believe in prayer; he did not believe in Christianity; he did not believe in his mother's Bible. This mother was a praying woman, and when she died, she left on earth a praying daughter. And when God saw her faith and heard that prayer, He answered her. How many sons and daughters could be saved if their mother and father had but faith?

At Murfreesboro, another similar story occurred. A young man received a letter from his mother, in which she said something like this: *My dear boy, you do not know how I am burdened for your salvation. Every morning and evening I go into my closet and pray for you, that you may be led to the cross of Christ. You may die in battle, or in the hospital, and oh, my son, I want you to become a Christian. I do not know but that this will be my last letter to you.*

This young lieutenant came to me and said, "I have just heard of my mother's death, and I have prayed for forgiveness of my sins." This young man was converted through his mother's faith. Although she was in glory, her voice was heard on earth.

God looks for faith among all who work for Him. He cannot do mighty things without it. With it He is able to do everything. Do you believe He is able to shake the world? Do you believe He is able to shake this country? Do you believe He is able to revive this area? Do you believe He is able to bring thousands into the kingdom of heaven?

New Sermons, Addresses, and Prayers of Dwight Lyman Moody

QUESTIONS TO CONSIDER
1. How might you increase your faith in God?
2. How can you use your faith for people in need?

A PRAYERFUL RESPONSE
Lord, show me the people I am to pray for in faith. Amen.

GOD IS ABLE

THOUGHT FOR TODAY

God is able to keep us standing strong in the faith.

WISDOM FROM SCRIPTURE

Who are you to judge someone else's servant? To his own master he stands or falls. And he will stand, for the Lord is able to make him stand.

One man considers one day more sacred than another; another man considers every day alike. Each one should be fully convinced in his own mind.

He who regards one day as special, does so to the Lord. He who eats meat, eats to the Lord, for he gives thanks to God; and he who abstains, does so to the Lord and gives thanks to God.

For none of us lives to himself alone and none of us dies to himself alone.

If we live, we live to the Lord; and if we die, we die to the Lord. So, whether we live or die, we belong to the Lord.

For this very reason, Christ died and returned to life so that he might be the Lord of both the dead and the living.

You, then, why do you judge your brother? Or why do you look down on your brother? For we will all stand before God's judgment seat.

It is written: "'As surely as I live,' says the Lord, 'every knee will bow before me; every tongue will confess to God.'"

So then, each of us will give an account of himself to God.

Therefore let us stop passing judgment on one another. Instead, make up your mind not to put any stumbling block or obstacle in your brother's way.

ROMANS 14:4-13, NIV

INSIGHTS FROM DWIGHT L. MOODY

When I first became a Christian, those who knew me predicted I would not hold out; that I would fall away in a few months. I used to fear and tremble myself; I was afraid I should fall. I knew nothing of the Bible; I was not acquainted with this precious Word. I don't think there were a dozen passages in the whole Word of God that I had committed to memory, which I could quote. I didn't know that God was able to make me stand.

But I have since learned the truth of it, and I tell you. If any of you are full of fear, full of doubt, and at times have actually trembled at the word *able*, it will hold you up in all your pilgrimage, in all your journey, no matter how rough and hard. God is able to make you stand.

The God who can create a world like this and call it from nothing into existence—the God who can create life with a word—He certainly can make a poor sinner like you and me "stand" by His mighty power. He was able to make Moses stand when exposed to the mighty temptations of Egypt. God enabled Daniel to stand in Babylon, when the whole city was against him. There he stood like a rock in the current of the river; the high, angry waves dashed up against him, but there he stood. He stood upright in that great city, with all against him. And Paul, I believe, wrote this blessed text out of his own experience. God held him up, and God made him stand. God sent him forth to the Gentiles, but along with him He sent His grace and gave him power from on high, telling him to be strong, to speak against the iniquity of men, and to testify against it.

And so, let me say, the God of Paul still lives; you have the same God Paul had. Oh, put your trust in God. Look to Him and pray to Him, and He will give you strength. He will make you stand. God has power enough; God has grace enough. God has strength enough to keep you on the straight path, if only you will look to Him, if only you will pray to Him daily for strength.

Let me warn you to put not your strength in yourself. When you are strong—when you think you are strong—then you are weak; that is the very time you are the weakest. Paul says, "When I am weak, then am I strong" (2 Cor 12:10). Our strength doesn't lie in ourselves; it lies in our Redeemer. If my strength is in myself, I will be constantly tumbling, constantly falling down. Therefore, keep a fast hold on God, who alone is able to make you stand.

I do not think a young convert will be able to stand by himself in a few years, or in many years. The stronger he gets, the stronger, too, grows the danger of his falling. The longer I live—the nearer I get to Christ—the more danger I see. The nearer a person draws to God, the more He constantly needs Him. Man never becomes independent of God, but the longer he lives the less confidence he should have in himself. In reading my Bible, I find that some of the most eminent men have fallen. They got self-confident, and when they became strong in themselves, they fell.

Let no Christian become spiritually proud and lifted up. He can come to no victory in his own strength. Let him pray, and then the tempter will go from him. You will find that people who have stood highest in the world have been people who have fallen, at different times, in their lives. I think you will find they stumbled on this stone of trusting in their own strength.

A great many temptations will assail you; a great many dangers await you. Should you be overcome, many who should help you may perhaps make sport of you and possibly point the finger of ridicule at you, instead of sympathizing with you as they ought. I pray you do not get discouraged. Instead of getting downhearted, go to God in prayer. Go to Him, for He is able to succor you in the hour of temptation. He has gone through it all. No one was more laughed at, no one more ridiculed, more scoffed at, more jeered at than the Son of God. Jesus can sympathize with you in all your hours of need.

Just ask for His help and He will succor you speedily. He will give you a glorious victory.

The Gospel Awakening

QUESTIONS TO CONSIDER
1. Today, how do you need God to "keep you standing"?
2. How will you know you are standing strong in faith?

A PRAYERFUL RESPONSE
Lord, keep me standing strong in You. Amen.

Wondrous Grace

Thought for Today
God supplies all the grace we need for any situation.

Wisdom From Scripture
Therefore, since we have a great high priest who has gone through the heavens, Jesus the Son of God, let us hold firmly to the faith we profess.

For we do not have a high priest who is unable to sympathize with our weaknesses, but we have one who has been tempted in every way, just as we are—yet was without sin.

Let us then approach the throne of grace with confidence, so that we may receive mercy and find grace to help us in our time of need.

Every high priest is selected from among men and is appointed to represent them in matters related to God, to offer gifts and sacrifices for sins.

He is able to deal gently with those who are ignorant and are going astray, since he himself is subject to weakness.

This is why he has to offer sacrifices for his own sins, as well as for the sins of the people.

No one takes this honor upon himself; he must be called by God, just as Aaron was.

So Christ also did not take upon himself the glory of becoming a high priest. But God said to him, "You are my Son; today I have become your Father."

And he says in another place, "You are a priest forever, in the order of Melchizedek."

During the days of Jesus' life on earth, he offered up prayers and petitions with loud cries and tears to the one who could save him from death, and he was heard because of his reverent submission.

Although he was a son, he learned obedience from what he suffered and, once made perfect, he became the source of eternal salvation for all who obey him.

HEBREWS 4:14–5:9, NIV

INSIGHTS FROM DWIGHT L. MOODY

Let us come boldly to the throne of grace. God wants us to come and get all the grace we need. The reason there are so many half-starved Christians is because they don't come to the throne of grace.

It is told about Alexander [the Great] that he gave one of his generals, who had pleased him, permission to draw on his treasurer for any sum. When the request came in, the treasurer was scared and wouldn't pay it till he saw his master. When the treasurer told him what the general had done, Alexander said, "Don't you know that he has honored me and my kingdom by making a large draft?"

So we honor God by making a large draft on Him. You can get enough to overcome every trial and sorrow. When Dr. Arnold was in this country, I heard him use a sermon illustration that impressed me. He said, "Haven't you ever been in a home where the family was at dinner, and haven't you seen the old family dog standing near and watching his master, and looking at every morsel of food as if he wished he had it? If the master drops a crumb, the dog at once licks it up, but if the master should set the dish of roast beef down and say, 'Come, come,' the dog wouldn't touch it— it's too much for him. So it is with God's children. They are willing to take a crumb but refuse when God wants them to go for the platter."

God wants you to come right to the throne of grace, and to come boldly. A while ago, I learned from the Chicago papers that there had been a run on the banks there, and many of them were broke. What a good thing it would be to get up a run on the bank of heaven! What a glorious thing to get up a run on the throne of grace! God is able to keep thee and deliver thee if you will only come to Him. That's what grace is for.

Now take all of the afflictions that the flesh is heir to, and all the troubles and trials of this life—no matter how numerous—and God has grace enough to carry you right through without a shadow. Some people borrow all the trouble they can from the past and the future, and then multiply it by ten, and get a big load, and go reeling and staggering under it. If you ask them to help anyone else, they say they can't—they've got enough to do to take care of their own, forgetting the verse, "Casting all your care upon Him, for He careth for you" (1 Pt 5:7).

So many are content to be nominal Christians and go along with great loads and burdens. What is the throne of grace for but to help you carry your burden? God says, "Come," and "As your day, so shall your strength be" (see Dt 33:25).

I suppose we all have thorns in the flesh. Instead of praying God to take the thorns out, let us pray for grace to bear them. Let us live day by day, casting our care upon God. Some think that when they get to Calvary, they have got it all. But they have just commenced. By and by we shall see the King in His beauty. The glory is just beyond.

A person said to me, "Moody, if God should take your

son, have you grace to bear it?"

I said, "What do I want grace for? I don't want grace to bear that which has not been sent. If God should call upon me to part with my boy, He would give me strength to bear it." What we want is grace for the present, to bear the trials and temptations for every day.

Christ pays the debt and gives us enough to live on besides. He doesn't merely pay our debt—He gives us enough to live on. He gives according to our need.

Rowland Hill tells a story of a rich man and a poor man of his congregation. The rich man came to Mr. Hill with a sum of money he wished to give to the poor man and asked Mr. Hill to give it to him as he thought best, either all at once or in small amounts. Mr. Hill sent the poor man a five-pound note with the endorsement: *More to follow.*

Now, which do you think did the most good? Every few months came the remittance with the same message: *More to follow.* Now that's grace. More to follow.

Yes, thank God, there is more to follow. Oh, wondrous grace!

Glad Tidings

QUESTIONS TO CONSIDER
1. For what do you need God's grace today?
2. How will this grace be evident in your life?

A PRAYERFUL RESPONSE
Lord, I accept Your full supply of grace for all that I need today. Amen.

DAY 26

THY WILL, NOT MINE

THOUGHT FOR TODAY

God's will is wiser than our own.

WISDOM FROM SCRIPTURE

I desire to do your will, O my God; your law is within my heart.

I proclaim righteousness in the great assembly; I do not seal my lips, as you know, O Lord.

I do not hide your righteousness in my heart; I speak of your faithfulness and salvation. I do not conceal your love and your truth from the great assembly.

Do not withhold your mercy from me, O Lord; may your love and your truth always protect me.

For troubles without number surround me; my sins have overtaken me, and I cannot see. They are more than the hairs of my head, and my heart fails within me.

Be pleased, O Lord, to save me; O Lord, come quickly to help me.

May all who seek to take my life be put to shame and confusion; may all who desire my ruin be turned back in disgrace.

May those who say to me, "Aha! Aha!" be appalled at their own shame.

But may all who seek you rejoice and be glad in you; may those who love your salvation always say, "The Lord be exalted!"

Yet I am poor and needy; may the Lord think of me. You are my help and my deliverer; O my God, do not delay.

PSALM 40:8-17, NIV

If we have spread our requests before the Lord, then we say, "Thy will be done." Keep that in mind. Often we set our wills against God's. That will be our ruin, perhaps. Let the will of God be done.

Submission! Submission! One of the sweetest lessons I have learned since I've been in Christ's school is just to be submissive and let Him choose for me. I tell Him what I want, but when I get through, I like to say, "Now Lord, you know best. Thy will be done."

I learned a lesson once from my little girl. She was always asking me for a great big doll. She had a lot of dolls around the house without heads, some without arms, some without legs, but she wanted a great big doll. If a man has an only daughter he is rather soft (and she finds it out, you know), and she was determined to get that big doll.

One day I had a good streak come over me, and I took her to a toy shop to get her a doll, but as we went in the door, we saw a basket of little china dolls.

"Oh, Papa, isn't that the cutest doll you ever saw?"

"Yes, yes."

"Well, won't you buy it?"

"Well, now, Emma, let me choose this time."

"Oh, no, Papa. I just want this little doll."

I paid a nickel for the doll and took her home. After the newness had worn off, the doll was left with all the others.

I said, "Emma, do you know what I was going to do that day when I took you into the toy shop, and you selected that little china doll?"

"No, Papa."

"Well, I was going to buy you one of those great big ones."

"You were? Why didn't you do it?"

"Because you wouldn't let me. You remember you wanted that little doll, and you had to have it."

She saw the point and bit her lip and did not say anything more. From that day to this, I cannot get her to say what she wants. When I was going to Europe the last time, I asked what she wanted me to bring her, and she said, "Anything you like."

It is far better to let God choose for us than to choose for ourselves.

"Thy will, not mine, be done."

Moody's Latest Sermons

QUESTIONS TO CONSIDER
1. Do you have fears or reservations about God's will for you? Explain.
2. How can you grasp that God's will is good?

A PRAYERFUL RESPONSE
Lord, I desire Your will, which is wiser than mine. Amen.

THE PASSIONATE WORK

Encamped along the hills of light,
Ye Christian soldiers, rise,
And press the battle ere the night
Shall veil the glowing skies.
Against the foes in vales below
Let all our strength be hurled;
Faith is the victory, we know,
That overcomes the world.
Faith is the victory!
Faith is the victory!
Oh, glorious victory,
That overcomes the world.

IRA D. SANKEY AND JOHN H. YATES

DWIGHT L. MOODY'S INSIGHT

When we receive God's unlimited grace, we desire to work passionately for Him.

DAY 27

Preach the Gospel

Thought for Today

The gospel affirms God's love for us.

Wisdom From Scripture

Now after he rose early on the first day of the week, he appeared first to Mary Magdalene, from whom he had cast out seven demons.

She went out and told those who had been with him, while they were mourning and weeping.

But when they heard that he was alive and had been seen by her, they would not believe it.

After this he appeared in another form to two of them, as they were walking into the country.

And they went back and told the rest, but they did not believe them.

Later he appeared to the eleven themselves as they were sitting at the table; and he upbraided them for their lack of faith and stubbornness, because they had not believed those who saw him after he had risen.

And he said to them, "Go into all the world and proclaim the good news to the whole creation.

"The one who believes and is baptized will be saved; but the one who does not believe will be condemned.

"And these signs will accompany those who believe: by using my name they will cast out demons; they will speak in new tongues; they will pick up snakes in their hands, and if they drink any deadly thing, it will not hurt them; they will lay their hands on the sick, and they will recover."

So then the Lord Jesus, after he had spoken to them, was taken up into heaven and sat down at the right hand of God.

And they went out and proclaimed the good news everywhere, while the Lord worked with them and confirmed the message by the signs that accompanied it.

Mark 16:9-20, NRSV

Insights From Dwight L. Moody

Christ had faced the world and conquered it. It was resting under His feet. He had met Satan and conquered him. He had met the Cross and conquered it. He had faced the enemy, which is death, and conquered it. He had gone down into the grave and had robbed the grave of its victory. Joseph's sepulcher lay behind Him now, empty. This is the captain of our salvation, sending out His warriors.

Around Him was gathered that handful of men who had been with Him in His ministry. You can see the tears trickling down their cheeks. He is now going to leave them. For three years—three short years, they must have been—they were in His company; they associated together. But now His work on earth was finished, as far as He was concerned. He must now go up on high and carry on the glorious work He had begun on earth.

In the sight of the world, the men around Him were weak and contemptible. There was not a mighty man among them. In the sight of the world they were unlettered, unlearned fishermen from Galilee, nearly all of them, and yet He sent them out as lambs among wolves. "Go ye into the world and preach the gospel to every creature." Don't leave out one.

Although the gospel has now been proclaimed for hundreds of years, and proclaimed in this country as in no other country under the sun—there is hardly a child who hasn't heard the gospel proclaimed. Yet I will venture to say there is not a word in the English language so little understood as the *gospel*. If I should ask this audience what the word means, there is not one out of ten who could tell. I think I had been a partaker of the gospel ten years before I knew what the word meant.

A great many people have an idea that the gospel is the most doleful message that ever came into this world; and when you begin to proclaim it, some people put on a face, as though you had brought a death warrant, or an invitation to attend some funeral or witness an execution, or go into some hospital where there is a plague. Many people act as if they were to be struck with a plague the moment you begin to talk to them about the gospel. The gospel of the Son of God is the best news that ever came from heaven to earth, the best news that was ever heard by mortals.

If people really believed it, we should not have to preach and preach, and coax them to believe it. It doesn't take people long to believe good news; but the fact is that the god of this world has blinded us, so that what is good news people think is bad news. When the angel came to the shepherds upon the plains of Bethlehem, the angel said unto them, "Fear not; for, behold, I bring you good tidings of great joy, which shall be to all people; for unto you is born this day in the city of David a Savior, who is Christ the Lord" (Lk 2:10-11). That is the gospel. God has provided a Savior for humanity.

When the world was lost and ruined, when there was no eye to pity, no hand to save, no one who could deliver, in the fullness of time God sent His own Son to redeem the world. That is the gospel. The word *gospel* means "God's spell." God is not imputing unto people their trespasses and sin, but seeking to forgive them, bringing good news, glad tidings of great joy. Who will believe it today and be saved?

For months before He died, Jesus told us that He was going up to Jerusalem to be delivered into the hands of the Gentiles, and He would be put to death, and on the third day He would rise again. For that purpose He came into the world, not only to live, but to die for the world, that through His death we might enter into eternal life.

Dwight Lyman Moody's Life Work and Gospel Sermons

QUESTIONS TO CONSIDER
1. How does your definition of the gospel compare to Moody's?
2. How can you share the gospel with others?

A PRAYERFUL RESPONSE
Lord, teach me how to share the gospel with Your world. Amen.

LOVE, THE POWER FOR SERVICE

THOUGHT FOR TODAY

The mark of the Christian is love.

WISDOM FROM SCRIPTURE

If I speak in the tongues of mortals and of angels, but do not have love, I am a noisy gong or a clanging cymbal.

And if I have prophetic powers, and understand all mysteries and all knowledge, and if I have all faith, so as to remove mountains, but do not have love, I am nothing.

If I give away all my possessions, and if I hand over my body so that I may boast, but do not have love, I gain nothing.

Love is patient; love is kind; love is not envious or boastful or arrogant or rude. It does not insist on its own way; it is not irritable or resentful; it does not rejoice in wrongdoing, but rejoices in the truth.

It bears all things, believes all things, hopes all things, endures all things.

Love never ends. But as for prophecies, they will come to an end; as for tongues, they will cease; as for knowledge, it will come to an end.

For we know only in part, and we prophesy only in part; but when the complete comes, the partial will come to an end.

When I was a child, I spoke like a child, I thought like a child, I reasoned like a child; when I became an adult, I put an end to childish ways.

For now we see in a mirror, dimly, but then we will see

face to face. Now I know only in part; then I will know fully, even as I have been fully known.

And now faith, hope, and love abide, these three; and the greatest of these is love.

1 CORINTHIANS 13, NRSV

INSIGHTS FROM DWIGHT L. MOODY

Christ gave His disciples a badge. Some of you wear a blue ribbon and others wear a red ribbon, but the badge that Christ gave to His disciples was love. "By this shall all men know that ye are my disciples, if ye have love one to another" (Jn 13:35). Love not only for those who are Christians, but love for the fallen.

The Good Samaritan had love for the poor man who had fallen among thieves. If we are filled with such love as that, the world will soon find out that we are the followers of the Lord Jesus Christ. It will do more to upset infidelity and rebellion against God than anything else.

I have a friend who has a large Sabbath school. He made up his mind when he began that if a boy did not have good training in his own home, he could not get it anywhere else except in the Sabbath school. He resolved that, if possible, when a boy was refractory he would not turn him adrift.

He had a boy come to the school whom no teacher seemed able to manage. One after another would come to the superintendent and say, "You must take him out of my class; he is demoralizing all the others. He uses profane language, and he is doing more harm than all the good I can do." At last my friend made up his mind that he would read the boy's name out and have him expelled publicly.

He told a few of the teachers what he was going to do, but a wealthy young lady said, "I wish you would let me try the boy. I will do all I can to win him." My friend said to himself he was sure she would not have patience with him for long, but he put the boy in her class as she requested. The little fellow soon broke the rules in the class, and she corrected him. He got so angry that he lost his temper and spat in her face. She quietly took a handkerchief and wiped off the spittle.

At the close of the lesson she asked him if he would walk home with her when school was over. No, he said, he didn't want to speak to her. He was not coming back to that old school any more. She asked if he would let her walk along with him. No, he wouldn't.

Well, she said, she was sorry he was going, but if he would call at her house on Tuesday morning and ring the front doorbell, there would be a little parcel waiting for him. She would not be at home herself, but if he asked the servant, he would receive it. He replied, "You can keep your old parcel. I don't want it." However, she thought he would be there.

By Tuesday morning the little fellow was over his fit. He came to the house and rang the doorbell; the servant handed him the parcel. When he opened it he found a little vest, a necktie, and best of all, a note written by the teacher. She told him how every night and every morning since he had been in her class she had been praying for him. Now that he was going to leave, she wanted him to remember that as long as she lived she would pray for him, and she hoped he would grow up to be a good man.

The next morning the little fellow was in the drawing room, waiting to see her before she came downstairs from her bedroom. She found him there, crying as if his heart would break. She asked him kindly what was the trouble.

"Oh," he said, "I have had no peace since I got your letter.

You have been so kind to me and I have been so unkind to you. I wish you would forgive me."

My friend the superintendent said later, "There are about eighteen hundred children in the school, and there is not a better boy among the whole of them."

Can we not do the same as that young lady did? Shall we not consecrate ourselves now to God and to His service?

Remember the words of Dr. Watts:

> Had I tongues of Greeks and Jews,
> And nobler speech than angels use;
> If love be absent, I am found
> Like tinkling brass, an empty sound.
> If love to God and love to men
> Be absent, all my hopes are vain;
> Nor tongues, nor gifts, nor fiery zeal,
> The work of love can e'er fulfill.

"To the Work! To the Work!"

QUESTIONS TO CONSIDER
1. Who, specifically, is difficult for you to love?
2. How can you express love to this person in practical ways?

A PRAYERFUL RESPONSE
Lord, let Your love flow through me. Amen.

A Call to Work

Thought for Today

We express our faith through our works.

Wisdom from Scripture

For the grace of God has appeared, bringing salvation to all, training us to renounce impiety and worldly passions, and in the present age to live lives that are self-controlled, upright, and godly, while we wait for the blessed hope and the manifestation of the glory of our great God and Savior, Jesus Christ.

He it is who gave himself for us that he might redeem us from all iniquity and purify for himself a people of his own who are zealous for good deeds.

Declare these things; exhort and reprove with all authority. Let no one look down on you.

Remind them to be subject to rulers and authorities, to be obedient, to be ready for every good work, to speak evil of no one, to avoid quarreling, to be gentle, and to show every courtesy to everyone.

For we ourselves were once foolish, disobedient, led astray, slaves to various passions and pleasures, passing our days in malice and envy, despicable, hating one another.

But when the goodness and loving kindness of God our Savior appeared, he saved us, not because of any works of righteousness that we had done, but according to his mercy, through the water of rebirth and renewal by the Holy Spirit.

This Spirit he poured out on us richly through Jesus

Christ our Savior, so that, having been justified by his grace, we might become heirs according to the hope of eternal life.

The saying is sure. I desire that you insist on these things, so that those who have come to believe in God may be careful to devote themselves to good works; these things are excellent and profitable to everyone.

TITUS 2:11–3:8, NRSV

INSIGHTS FROM DWIGHT L. MOODY

The Word of God won't amount to anything unless we put two things together: Word and work—the two W's. You will soon get spiritually gorged if it is all Word and no work. If you want to be a healthy Christian, your life must include both Word and work.

If we can get people to work, how rapidly they will grow. My experience is that a man or woman who is engaged in the Lord's work and feeding on the Bible is growing all the while. Whoever is not working is sure to become stunted. The Christian life means progress and growth.

If every Christian man and woman would sincerely pray, "Lord, what will You have me to do?" what a mighty work would be accomplished! If you have a heart for the work, God will qualify you. There will be no trouble about your finding something to do.

If each one of us is doing some little thing, it isn't little in the Master's sight. If we keep at it 365 days in the year, there will be a good deal of work done at the end of the year. The people who have been permitted to do higher things are the people who began with small things. If you are not willing to deal with one person about his soul, and labor with that one person, you are not fit to go into the pulpit and preach to others. Some of Christ's greatest discourses were given to one or two persons. He preached the great sermon on regeneration to Nicodemus. He delivered that wonderful sermon at the well when the disciples were off to the city—delivered to one poor, fallen woman. Don't wait for something to turn up, but go and turn up something.

There are a great many different ways of doing good. A lady once visited a hospital and noticed with what pleasure the patients would smell and look at the flowers sent to them. She said, "If I had known that a bunch of flowers would do so much good, I would have sent some from home." As soon as she got home, she sent some flowers out of her garden. It was a little thing—a bouquet of flowers. It was a very insignificant work—very small. But if it is done in the right spirit, God accepts it. A cup of water given in His name is accepted as given to Himself. Nothing that is done for God is small.

When Elijah sent his servant to see if there was any sign of rain, and when the servant saw the cloud no bigger than a man's hand, perhaps he thought it was a very insignificant thing. But Elijah knew what it meant; and he told the man to go and warn Ahab that he had better make haste and get home, or he would get a good drenching before he got there. Elijah knew God was in the cloud. Anything God is in isn't small.

If we go to work right at home we will have success. Every child of God can do something, if he will. If you can't get grown people, get the children. If you can't get people to church, go to their homes. Hold meetings in schoolhouses. Go up into the mountains and visit the families. You don't have to wait until you are ordained. If He is the vine and we are the branches, we are going to bring forth fruit. Make up your mind that you are going to bring forth fruit.

When I was in London, an old woman of eighty-five came and begged to be given something to do. I gave her a district, and how joyfully she took it and went to work. People who would have closed the door on a young man wouldn't close the door on an old woman. If everyone would do as much as she did, what a difference there would be! I find a good many people as I travel over this country who never know what it is to be spiritually cold—never know what is it to be lukewarm. Why? Because they are working for the Lord all the while.

Thank God, we have all eternity to rest. This life is the place to work. I pity any child of God who wants to sleep all the time down here. Brothers and sisters, wake up! We have plenty of time to rest hereafter. The question is not what Gabriel can do, or what we will do when we get to heaven. The question is, what can you and I do before we get there?

The Home Work of D.L. Moody

QUESTIONS TO CONSIDER
1. How do we know we are called to work for God?
2. What "small" work can you begin doing for Him?

A PRAYERFUL RESPONSE
Lord, I will answer Your call to work, no matter how small the task. Amen.

DAY 30

Work for Everyone

Thought for Today

God has specific work for each one of us to do.

Wisdom from Scripture

[Jesus said,] "From the fig tree learn its lesson: as soon as its branch becomes tender and puts forth its leaves, you know that summer is near.

"So also, when you see these things taking place, you know that he is near, at the very gates.

"Truly I tell you, this generation will not pass away until all these things have taken place.

"Heaven and earth will pass away, but my words will not pass away.

"But about that day or hour no one knows, neither the angels in heaven, nor the Son, but only the Father.

"Beware, keep alert; for you do not know when the time will come.

"It is like a man going on a journey, when he leaves home and puts his slaves in charge, each with his work, and commands the doorkeeper to be on the watch.

"Therefore, keep awake—for you do not know when the master of the house will come, in the evening, or at midnight, or at cockcrow, or at dawn, or else he may find you asleep when he comes suddenly.

"And what I say to you I say to all: Keep awake."

MARK 13:28-37, NRSV

Insights From Dwight L. Moody

This verse doesn't read, "to every one some work," or "to every one person a work," but to "each his work." I believe, if the truth be known, that every man and woman has a work laid out for him or her to do. Every person's life is a plan of the Almighty, and way back in the councils of eternity God laid out a work for each one of us.

There is no person living who can do the work God has for me to do. No one can do it but myself. And if the work isn't done, I will answer for it when I stand before God. For the Bible says that every man shall be brought into judgment, and everyone shall give an account of the deeds done in the body. And it seems to me that every one of us ought to take this question home: "Am I doing the work God has for me to do?"

God has a work for each one of us to do. In one of Jesus' parables, a man who had two talents had the same reward as the man who had five talents. He heard the same words as the man who had been given five talents: "Well done, thou good and faithful servant, enter thou into the joy of thy Lord" (Mt 25:21).

When people take good care of the talents God has loaned them, He always gives them more. But if we take the talent God has given us and lay it away carefully in a napkin and bury it away, God will take even that from us. God doesn't want a person who has one talent to do the work of a person who has ten. All a person has to answer for is the talent God has given to him or her. If we were doing the work God has for us to do, don't we see how the work of the Lord would advance? I believe in what John Wesley used to say, "All at it, and always at it," and that is what the church wants today.

What is our purpose in this world of sickness and sorrow

unless it is to work for the Son of God and improve the talents He has given us? Some people are not satisfied with the talents they have, but are always wishing for someone else's talents. Now that is all wrong. It is contrary to the Spirit of Christ. Instead of wishing for someone else's talents, let us make the best use of the talents God has given us.

There isn't a father or mother who wouldn't think it a great misfortune if their children didn't grow any for the next ten or fifteen years. Yet I know some people who say the same prayers they said fifteen or twenty years ago. They are like a horse on a treadmill going round and round. It is always the same old story of their experiences when they were converted.

If you had a child who was deaf and dumb, you would think it a great misfortune. Do you ever think how many deaf and dumb children God has? You speak about political matters, and they can talk. But you ask them to talk about the Son of God, and they say, "Oh, no, I can't speak about that. Please excuse me." Either they don't believe, or they have done like the man who buried his talent, and they say, "The Lord is a hard master." The people who bury their talents think the Lord is a hard master, but the people who are using their talents think no such thing.

Let us do all the business we can. If we can't be a lighthouse, let us be a tallow candle. There used to be a time when people came to meetings bringing their candles with them. The first person with a candle, perhaps, wouldn't make a great illumination, but when two or three got there, there would be more light. If the people of this city should do that now, if each one should come here with a candle, don't you think there would be light? Let all the gas be put out in this hall, and one solitary candle would be a good deal of light. If we can't be a lighthouse, let us be a tallow candle.

Someone said, "I can't be anything more than a farthing rushlight." If you can't be more, be that. That is enough. Be all you can.

If God has given us but half a talent, let us make good use of that. When Jesus told the people to take their seats by fifties, He told Philip to get food for them.

"What?" said Philip. "Feed them with this little loaf? There is not more than enough for the first person."

Philip thought that was a very small amount for such a multitude. He broke off a piece for the first person and didn't miss it. A piece for the second person and didn't miss it. A piece for the third person and didn't miss it. He was making good use of the loaf, and God kept increasing it. That is what the Lord wants to do with us. He will give us just as many talents as we can take care of.

There are many of us willing to do great things for the Lord, but few of us are willing to do little things. There are many who are willing to preach to thousands but are not willing to take a seat beside one soul and lead that one to the blessed Jesus. We must get down to personal effort—bringing people, one by one, to the Son of God.

Glad Tidings

QUESTIONS TO CONSIDER
1. What talent has God given to you?
2. How can you employ that talent in work for God?

A PRAYERFUL RESPONSE
Lord, as I use my talent for Your work, please multiply its effectiveness. Amen.

THE HOLY SPIRIT'S WORK

THOUGHT FOR TODAY

To be effective in God's work, we need the Holy Spirit's power.

WISDOM FROM SCRIPTURE

In the first book, Theophilus, I wrote about all that Jesus did and taught from the beginning until the day when he was taken up to heaven, after giving instructions through the Holy Spirit to the apostles whom he had chosen.

After his suffering he presented himself alive to them by many convincing proofs, appearing to them during forty days and speaking about the kingdom of God.

While staying with them, he ordered them not to leave Jerusalem, but to wait there for the promise of the Father. "This," he said, "is what you have heard from me; for John baptized with water, but you will be baptized with the Holy Spirit not many days from now."

So when they had come together, they asked him, "Lord, is this the time when you will restore the kingdom to Israel?"

He replied, "It is not for you to know the times or periods that the Father has set by his own authority.

"But you will receive power when the Holy Spirit has come upon you; and you will be my witnesses in Jerusalem, in all Judea and Samaria, and to the ends of the earth."

ACTS 1:1-8, NRSV

Insights From Dwight L. Moody

Isn't it a time of need, great need? I think one of the most lamentable things of this day is that Satan can walk right into some of our best Christian homes and families and haul the children down into the deepest and darkest depths, and we haven't the power to reach them and bring them back. I don't believe that is the will of the Almighty, that the devil should walk into my home and drag my children down.

If we were filled with the Holy Spirit, we could call power down from heaven and save the tempted ones. We don't have Holy Ghost power. May God open our eyes now! Perhaps the question comes up, is there any promise about this power that we can lay hold on?

Listen: "Blessed are they that do hunger and thirst after righteousness, for they shall be filled" (Mt 5:6). Do you know what heaven's measure is? Good measure pressed down and running over (see Lk 6:38). I remember when we used to sell a bushel of oats; we used to take a stick and scrape over the top so the buyer wouldn't get a grain over measure. The Lord just shakes it down and lets it run over, and when a person is full of the love of God, he has the power to resist temptation. When the heart is filled with the Holy Spirit, and Satan comes to put in an evil thought, he throws off the temptation.

People come to me and say, "Mr. Moody, don't you think you ought to preach against this and that?"

"No," I say. "Get the people baptized and it takes them out of the world."

A young man came to me once and said, "Don't you think I ought to get out of the world now that I have become a Christian?"

I said, "No, you won't have to leave the world if you just give a good ringing testimony for the Son of God."

God wants to fill you. But the moment you begin to talk about being filled, people say, "If you are full of conceit and your own righteousness, full of envy, evil, and hate, and all those things, how is the Lord going to fill you?"

Say to God, "Here I am." And if it is a real, honest desire that He should come, He will do so and fill you.

When the Spirit of God is in a person, the fire just burns. But, thank God, although Samson lost his strength, it came back to him. And some of you Samsons who have lost your power can get it back again if you will ask. God used Peter far more after He restored him than He did before his fall.

I trust there are some who may become a flame of fire. Why not? Don't you want that power? You can have it if you will. It is for you. The Lord wants to give it to everyone. Let's have it.

You will remember that after Christ rose, He met His disciples in a little room, and He raised His pierced hands and said, "Receive ye the Holy Spirit" (Jn 20:22). And right after that He said, "I am going to leave you, and I want to come back here and pray until you have become imbued with power from on high."

One of His disciples answered, "Lord, I have the power." And then He said, "Ye shall receive power, after the Holy Spirit is come upon you" (Acts 1:8).

You need to wait for the power. I believe that is where the church has gone astray; there are hundreds of church members who never think of asking God for power. They are children by birth, sons and daughters of God, but they are without power. Let us seek His power.

When the Holy Spirit had come, there were more people converted than had been during the three years of Christ's ministry. Oh, I hope Christians will get power and the baptism, and then whole communities will feel the power.

"Blessed are they that hunger and thirst after righteousness, for they shall be filled." Claim that promise. God can raise up witnesses right out of stone if He wants to. Elisha got all he went for because he dared to ask. Let us go in for a double portion. Don't you want it?

What is the use of living at this dying rate? The Lord has plenty. He delights to give. Let us take up the duty of receiving just now. Let us pray the Lord God of heaven to fill us. Let us pray to have the fruit come.

Moody's Latest Sermons

QUESTIONS TO CONSIDER
1. Do you feel the Holy Spirit's power in your life? Explain.
2. Are you willing to ask God for more spiritual power? Why, or why not?

A PRAYERFUL RESPONSE
Lord, fill me with Your Holy Spirit and power. Amen.

Working With Enthusiasm

Thought for Today

Engaging in God's work wakes up the worker's spiritual life.

Wisdom from Scripture

"Sleeper, awake! Rise from the dead, and Christ will shine on you."

Be careful then how you live, not as unwise people but as wise, making the most of the time, because the days are evil.

So do not be foolish, but understand what the will of the Lord is.

Do not get drunk with wine, for that is debauchery; but be filled with the Spirit, as you sing psalms and hymns and spiritual songs among yourselves, singing and making melody to the Lord in your hearts, giving thanks to God the Father at all times and for everything in the name of our Lord Jesus Christ.

Be subject to one another out of reverence for Christ.

Ephesians 5:14-21, NRSV

Insights from Dwight L. Moody

When we as children of God wake up and go to work in the vineyard, then those who are living in wickedness all about us will be reached, but not in any other way. You may go to mass meetings and discuss the question of how to reach the masses, but when you are done with the discussion, you have to go back to personal effort. Every man and woman who loves the Lord Jesus Christ must wake up to the fact that he or she has a mission in the world, in this work of reaching the lost.

There is no better way to wake up a church than to set it to work. One person will wake up another. Of course, the moment we begin a work and declare war with the world, the flesh and the devil, some wise head will begin to shake, and there will be the cry, "Zeal without knowledge!" I think I have heard that objection ever since I began the Christian life.

I heard of someone who was speaking of something that was to be done, and who said he hoped zeal would be tempered with moderation. Another friend very wisely replied that he hoped moderation would be tempered with zeal. If that were always the case, Christianity would be like a red-hot ball rolling over the face of the earth. There is no power on earth that can stand before the onward march of God's people when they are in dead earnest.

God always uses those who are in earnest. Satan always calls idle men into his service. God calls active and earnest, not indolent men. When we are thoroughly ready for His work, then He will take us up and use us. You remember where Elijah found Elisha; he was plowing in the field—he was at work. Gideon was at the threshing floor. Moses was away in Horeb, looking after the sheep. None of these eminent servants of God were indolent men; what they did, they did with all their might. We want such men and women nowadays. If we cannot do God's work with all the knowledge we would like, let us at any rate do it with all the zeal God has given us.

A good many people are afraid of the word *enthusiasm*. Do you know what the word means? It means "in God." The person who is "in God" will surely be fired with enthusiasm. When a person goes into business filled with fire and zeal, he will generally carry everyone with him. In the army a general who is full of enthusiasm will fire up his troops and will accomplish a great deal more than one who is not stirred with the same spirit.

People say that if we go on with zeal, then many mistakes will be made. Probably that is true. You never saw any boy learning a trade who did not make a good many mistakes. If you do not go to work because you are afraid of making mistakes, you will probably make one great mistake—the greatest mistake of your life—that of doing nothing. If we all do what we can, then a good deal will be accomplished.

God wants men and women; they are far better than institutions. If men or women are really in earnest, they will not wait to be put on some committee. If I saw a man fall into a river, and he was in danger of drowning, I would not wait until I was placed on some committee before I tried to save him. Many people say they cannot work because they have not been formally appointed. Let us look on the whole world as our parish, as a great harvest field.

If God puts anyone within our influence, let us tell him of Christ and heaven. The world may rise up and say that we are mad. In my opinion, no one is fit for God's service until he is willing to be considered mad by the world. They said Paul was mad. I wish we had many more who were bitten with the same kind of madness. As someone has said, "If we are mad, we have a good Keeper on the way and a good asylum at the end of the road."

One great trouble is that people come to special revival meetings, and for two or three weeks, perhaps, they will keep to the fire, but by and by it dies out. They are like a bundle of shavings with kerosene on the top—they blaze away for a little time, but soon there is nothing left. We want to keep ablaze all the time—morning, noon, and night.

I heard of a well of water that was said to be very good, except that it had two faults. It would freeze up in the winter and dry up in the summer. A most extraordinary well, but I am afraid there are many wells like it. There are many people who are good at certain times; as someone has expressed it, they seem to be good "in spots." What we want is to be red-hot all the time.

Do not wait until someone hunts you up. People talk about striking while the iron is hot. I believe it was Cromwell who said that he would rather strike the iron and make it hot. So let us keep at our post, and we will soon grow warm in the Lord's work.

What we want today is the spirit of consecration and concentration. May God pour out His spirit upon us and fill us with a holy enthusiasm.

"To the Work! To the Work!"

QUESTIONS TO CONSIDER
1. What image does the word *zeal* bring to your mind? How do you feel about it?
2. How might you increase your enthusiasm for God's work?

A PRAYERFUL RESPONSE
Lord, fill me with Your zeal for reaching those who don't know You. Amen.

DAY 33

Serving With Perseverance

Thought for Today

Those who persevere in the Lord's work reap spiritual success.

Wisdom From Scripture

If we live by the Spirit, let us also be guided by the Spirit.

Let us not become conceited, competing against one another, envying one another.

My friends, if anyone is detected in a transgression, you who have received the Spirit should restore such a one in a spirit of gentleness. Take care that you yourselves are not tempted.

Bear one another's burdens, and in this way you will fulfill the law of Christ.

For if those who are nothing think they are something, they deceive themselves.

All must test their own work; then that work, rather than their neighbor's work, will become a cause for pride.

For all must carry their own loads.

Those who are taught the word must share in all good things with their teacher.

Do not be deceived; God is not mocked, for you reap whatever you sow.

If you sow to your own flesh, you will reap corruption from the flesh; but if you sow to the Spirit, you will reap eternal life from the Spirit.

So let us not grow weary in doing what is right, for we will reap at harvest time, if we do not give up.

So then, whenever we have an opportunity, let us work for the good of all, and especially for those of the family of faith.

GALATIANS 5:25–6:10, NRSV

INSIGHTS FROM DWIGHT L. MOODY

I want to draw your attention to the necessity of perseverance, if we are going to be successful in the vineyard of the Lord. I believe many fail because they don't persevere.

It isn't the man or woman who works for only a few weeks, and then gives up, who reaps. It is those who work on day and night and hold on to the work. "We shall reap," says the promise, "if we faint not." I haven't yet found the man or woman who has been at work for the Lord and kept persevering who has not been successful. It may take weeks, it may take months, and it may take years, but they have His promise. "We shall reap."

Some people tell us that we do not work enough. I presume there is a good deal of truth in it. I have little hope where men and women are roused up to work only for a few weeks, and if this is all these meetings do, they will be a failure. What we want to do is persevere, and remember that we have the word of the Lord that we shall reap.

Faith is an act of the mind, but work is an outward sign of faith. You can't have true faith without having works, no more than you can have fire without heart. If a person tells me he has faith in Jesus Christ but no impulse to work for God, I doubt his word. I would not give much for his faith, because if he has faith and believes on the Lord Jesus Christ, he cannot help working for Him.

It is just as much a command for a person to work after a confession of faith as it is to remember the Sabbath day.

Laziness doesn't belong to the new creation; it belongs to the old. If a person professes to be converted and is not stirred up to work for God, I doubt the conversion. He may make great professions, but if he has no desire to work for God, it's a true sign that he has not been born of God.

I was for twelve or fifteen years superintendent of a Sabbath school in the mission district of Chicago, and you know it isn't easy work in these districts. It is sometimes very dark and discouraging, when you have doubtless been pulling seven days in the week, and perhaps the children's parents have been doing all they could to prevent you from your work. It is sometimes pretty dark, like fishing all night and not catching anything.

I noticed that the people who got discouraged and gave up their classes, and went from one school to another, from one field to another, were never successful. But those who persevered and held on, day after day, week after week, month after month—those who held right on, have always been blessed.

We find there are some Christians who are fruitful, others who have to be pruned, and that makes them more fruitful; but those who abide in Christ bring forth much fruit. We are not going into the world after comfort, but to abide in Christ and get strength and power to serve Him. If we want to be faithful and bring forth one hundred-fold, we should abide in Him. God can make us successful if we are willing to be doers of the Word as well as hearers.

In James 1:22 we read, "But be ye doers of the word and not hearers only, deceiving your own selves." If we are going to have pure religion, we have to be something besides hearers of the Word; we have to be doers of it. And if I can only say something to stir up thousands of Christians to be doers of the Word, don't you see how the influence of this could spread, and how many hundreds would feel its influence before long, and how many would be won to Christ?

Suppose all the Christians here this morning were watching for souls and talked to someone near them, what an influence they would have. You can generally tell who the Christians are by their eyes and manners—their faces shine. If all the Christians in this city would unite in the work, there would be a great army to work for Christ. I don't know why we shouldn't have thousands of these workers. What a blessed and glorious privilege to lead a soul out of the darkness into the light.

"To all People"

QUESTIONS TO CONSIDER
1. What obstacles could keep you from persevering in God's work for you?
2. How can you overcome these obstacles?

A PRAYERFUL RESPONSE
Lord, I want to reap the rewards of persevering in Your work. Amen.

COURAGE IN THE LORD'S WORK

THOUGHT FOR TODAY

Putting our confidence in the Lord, we can have courage in spiritual battle.

WISDOM FROM SCRIPTURE

After the death of Moses the servant of the Lord, the Lord spoke to Joshua son of Nun, Moses' assistant, saying, "My servant Moses is dead. Now proceed to cross the Jordan, you and all this people, into the land that I am giving to them, to the Israelites.

"Every place that the sole of your foot will tread upon I have given to you, as I promised to Moses.

"From the wilderness and the Lebanon as far as the great river, the river Euphrates, all the land of the Hittites, to the Great Sea in the west shall be your territory.

"No one shall be able to stand against you all the days of your life. As I was with Moses, so I will be with you; I will not fail you or forsake you.

"Be strong and courageous; for you shall put this people in possession of the land that I swore to their ancestors to give them.

"Only be strong and very courageous, being careful to act in accordance with all the law that my servant Moses commanded you; do not turn from it to the right hand or to the left, so that you may be successful wherever you go.

"This book of the law shall not depart out of your mouth; you shall meditate on it day and night, so that you may be careful to act in accordance with all that is written in it. For then you shall make your way prosperous, and then you shall be successful.

"I hereby command you: Be strong and courageous; do not be frightened or dismayed, for the Lord your God is with you wherever you go."

JOSHUA 1:1-9, NRSV

INSIGHTS FROM DWIGHT L. MOODY

The Lord told Joshua, "I will not forsake thee or fail thee." That is, if Joshua went into the battle not thinking of himself or depending upon somebody else, but relying upon the Lord. So it is with us.

If we go into battle and look on the weak side, we are going to lose. We must fight with the courage of a Joshua. I have learned one thing since I went into the school of Christ. That is, God never takes a man for His purposes who is weak; he must have confidence in himself through Christ; must not hang on to his own strength, but must have courage, and must believe that God is willing and ready to aid him.

God will not have a person in His service He cannot control and who is thrown down by the slightest opposition. We must act as Joshua did when he went out, I suppose, to view the lines. All at once a man stood before him with a drawn sword. If Joshua had not heard the words of the Lord, and had the fear of God in his heart, he would have run away. Instead, he stood boldly and confronted God's messenger, and asked, "Art thou for us or against us?"

"Nay," said the man, "I come as the captain of the host of the Lord, to lead you to victory." And so, if obstacles stand before us, we must have courage if we wish success.

Look at Elijah's courage when he stood before Ahab, when he defied the priests of Baal on Mount Carmel. I don't know what came over him when Jezebel sent him that messenger and nearly scared him out of his wits. He stood like a lion on Mount Carmel, but look at him when he received the letter—how he ran away into the wilderness, and sat down under a juniper tree. He despaired utterly. He thought he had lived long enough and asked the Lord to let him die. So it is with some of us. The first thing that frightens us, and we fly under a juniper tree. God wants us to have courage and faith in Him.

Look at Gideon, with his thirty-two thousand men, which looked like a large army. But the Lord said, "You have many men there." He wanted the force cut down. A great many of those men had fears and doubts—they did not feel confident in God's power. God does not work in this way. So Gideon drew his army up to a line and said, "All those who are afraid, step out of this line." I can imagine the weak ones saying, "This is a good chance to get home, and we will not get shot." And twenty-two thousand stepped out.

But the Lord said, "Too many yet." And Gideon drew them up again and said, "All you who are afraid, step out," and his army was reduced to three hundred. I can imagine some of them saying, "Gideon has made a mistake doing this," but Gideon knew what he was about.

If we could just whittle down our numbers like Gideon and believe that if the Lord is present, a few is just as good as many. Small numbers make no difference to God. There is nothing small that God is in. People say Gideon must have trembled when he saw his army reduced to three hundred men, but he knew that if God was with that little band, it was more powerful than one hundred thousand men.

Dear friends, let us have courage and believe that God can accomplish all things; and if the Spirit of God prompts you to go and speak to that young man—if the Spirit urges you to write a letter to a friend about Christ—have the courage to do it. Speak to them in the name of the Master. If three hundred men like Gideon's band are found in this audience, this city will be converted—three hundred who are willing to lay everything upon the altar and take up the Cross of Christ. He will take us up and use us.

John Wesley used to say that if he had one hundred men who heard God, and were true to Jesus, he could shake the gates of hell. We want men and women who have confidence in the old gospel of Jesus Christ. There is as much power in the Word today as ever there was, and people need the gospel just as much as they ever needed it.

To wait for results we must have patience, we must have courage, and God will help us. Pray to God that He will give us the moral courage to fight the glorious battle.

New Sermons, Addresses, and Prayers of Dwight Lyman Moody

QUESTIONS TO CONSIDER
1. For what do you need spiritual courage?
2. How could you build yourself up in God's courage?

A PRAYERFUL RESPONSE
Lord, because I trust You, I will be courageous in the spiritual battle. Amen.

DAY 35

THE REWARD OF THE FAITHFUL

THOUGHT FOR TODAY
God rewards those who work for Him.

WISDOM FROM SCRIPTURE
Meanwhile the disciples were urging him, "Rabbi, eat something."

But he said to them, "I have food to eat that you do not know about."

So the disciples said to one another, "Surely no one has brought him something to eat?"

Jesus said to them, "My food is to do the will of him who sent me and to complete his work.

"Do you not say, 'Four months more, then comes the harvest'? But I tell you, look around you, and see how the fields are ripe for harvesting.

"The reaper is already receiving wages and is gathering fruit for eternal life, so that sower and reaper may rejoice together.

"For here the saying holds true, 'One sows and another reaps.'

"I sent you to reap that for which you did not labor. Others have labored, and you have entered into their labor."

Many Samaritans from that city believed in him because of the woman's testimony, "He told me everything I have ever done."

So when the Samaritans came to him, they asked him to stay with them; and he stayed there two days.

And many more believed because of his word.

JOHN 4:31-41, NRSV

157

Insights From Dwight L. Moody

"He that reapeth receiveth wages." I can speak from experience. I have been in the Lord's service for twenty-one years, and I want to testify that He is a good paymaster—that He pays promptly. To go out and labor for Him—to guide a poor, weary soul to the way of life and turn his face toward the golden gates of Zion—is a thing to be proud of.

The Lord's wages are better than silver and gold, because He says the loyal soul shall receive a crown of glory. Here is a proclamation coming directly from the throne of grace to every man, woman, and child to gather into God's vineyard, where they will find treasures that never fade, and these treasures will be crowns of everlasting life. The laborer will find treasures laid up in his Father's house, and after serving faithfully here, he will be greeted by friends assembled there.

Work for tens of thousands of men, women, and children! Think of it and of the reward. Little children are apt to be overlooked, but they must be led to Christ. Children have done a great deal in the vineyard. They have led parents to Jesus. It was a little girl who led Naaman to Christ. Christ can find useful work for these little ones. He can see little things, and we ought to pay great attention to them. If I could only impress upon you that we have come to a vineyard, to reap and to gather, we shall have a glorious harvest.

The Lord must teach us what our work shall be. Let every child of God say, "Teach me, God, what I can do to help these men and women to the way of salvation." Take the gospel of the Lord to them. Tell them what to do with it.

Think of the privilege, my friend, of saving a soul. If we are going to work for the good, we must be up and about it. Some say, "I have no time." Take it. Ten minutes every day for Christ will give you good wages. Some of you with silver locks, I hear you saying, "I wish I were young, how I would rush into the battle." If you cannot be a fighter, you can pray and lead on the others.

There are two kinds of people in the world. One grows chilled and sour, and the other lights up every meeting with a genial presence and cheers on the workers. Draw near, old age, and cheer on the others, and take them by the hand and encourage them.

There was a building on fire. The flames leaped around the staircase, and from a three-story window a little child was seen who cried for help. The only way to reach the child was by a ladder. One was obtained and a fireman ascended, but when he had almost reached the child, the flames broke from the window and leaped around him. He faltered and seemed afraid to go further. Suddenly someone in the crowd shouted, "Give him a cheer," and cheer after cheer went up. The fireman was filled with new energy and rescued the child.

Just so with our young people. Whenever you see them wavering, cheer them on. If you cannot go yourself, give them cheers to move them on in their glorious work. May the blessing of God fall upon us, and let every man and woman be up and doing.

Great Joy

QUESTIONS TO CONSIDER
1. What spiritual rewards have you already received from the Lord?
2. What rewards do you still wish to receive? Why?

A PRAYERFUL RESPONSE
Lord, thank You for bestowing spiritual rewards upon me. Amen.

DAY 36

TIME FOR REVIVAL

THOUGHT FOR TODAY
God will do what it takes to revive His people spiritually.

WISDOM FROM SCRIPTURE
Lord, you were favorable to your land; you restored the fortunes of Jacob.

You forgave the iniquity of your people; you pardoned all their sin.

You withdrew all your wrath; you turned from your hot anger.

Restore us again, O God of our salvation, and put away your indignation toward us.

Will you be angry with us forever? Will you prolong your anger to all generations?

Will you not revive us again, so that your people may rejoice in you?

Show us your steadfast love, O Lord, and grant us your salvation.

Let me hear what God the Lord will speak, for he will speak peace to his people, to his faithful, to those who turn to him in their hearts.

Surely his salvation is at hand for those who fear him, that his glory may dwell in our land.

Steadfast love and faithfulness will meet; righteousness and peace will kiss each other.

Faithfulness will spring up from the ground, and righteousness will look down from the sky.

The Lord will give what is good, and our land will yield its increase.

Righteousness will go before him, and will make a path for his steps.

PSALM 85, NRSV

INSIGHTS FROM DWIGHT L. MOODY

Revivals and awakenings are perfectly scriptural. In all ages God has been quickening His people.

There was a mighty awakening when Moses was sent down into Egypt to bring the children of Israel out of the house of bondage. From Moses right on down, whenever Israel went back into idolatry, God raised up prophets and people of God to bring the nation back to Him.

I used to think I would like to have lived in the days of the prophets, but I have gotten over that. The prophets appeared on the scene only when everything was dark as midnight and Israel had fallen away from the worship of Jehovah to serve the gods of the nations around them. Then God used the prophets to call His people back.

It was dark when Samuel appeared. Eli's family had gone astray, the ark of God had fallen into the hands of the enemy, and everything was dark. First Samuel 7:3-4 says, "And Samuel spoke unto all the house of Israel, saying, if ye do return unto the Lord with all your hearts, then put away the foreign gods and Ashtaroth from among you, and prepare your hearts unto the Lord, and serve Him only; and he will deliver you out of the hand of the Philistines. Then the children of Israel did put away Baalim and Ashtaroth, and served the Lord only."

Then in the eleventh verse we see the result: Israel smote its enemies. It has always been so in history. Whenever people have repented and put away their idols and served God only, then God has come with mighty power and driven out the enemy.

In the days of Elijah, midnight darkness had settled upon the land, and God used him to bring about a mighty revival. God raised up Jeremiah to draw the people back, and some heard his voice and took warning, but others persisted in living in their sins. The result was that they went into captivity.

When God has revived His work, there has always been great need; it is darkest just before the dawn. I think it is getting very dark, but don't think for a moment that I am a pessimist. I haven't any more doubt about the final outcome of things than I have of my existence. I believe Jesus is going to sway His scepter to the ends of the earth, that the time is coming when God's will is to be done on earth as it is in heaven, and when a person's voice will be only the echo of God's. I believe the time is coming when every knee will bow and every tongue will confess Christ.

I am no pessimist, and I am not under the juniper tree, either. If I look on the dark side, it is to stir you up and get you fighting. But it is getting dark, there is no doubt about that. Paul says in his second letter to Timothy, "This know, also, that in the last days perilous times shall come. For men shall be lovers of their own selves, covetous, boasters, proud, blasphemers, disobedient to parents, unthankful, unholy, without natural affection, trucebreakers, false accusers, incontinent, fierce, despisers of those that are good" (2 Tm 3:1-3).

Do we not need a reformation? Hasn't the time come for the children of God to cry out, "Oh, God, revive Thy work!"

Moody's Latest Sermons

QUESTIONS TO CONSIDER
1. Do you sense a need for revival in your heart?
2. How does personal revival begin?

A PRAYERFUL RESPONSE
Lord, bring revival to my heart so I can help revive others. Amen.

THE HOPE OF HEAVEN

Under His wings, O what precious enjoyment!
There will I hide till life's trials are o'er;
Sheltered, protected, no evil can harm me;
Resting in Jesus I'm safe evermore.
Under His wings, under His wings,
Who from His love can sever?
Under His wings my soul shall abide,
Safely abide forever.

IRA D. SANKEY AND WILLIAM O. CUSHING

DWIGHT L. MOODY'S INSIGHT
No matter our circumstances on earth, we can cling to the
certain hope of heaven.

THE BLESSED HOPE

THOUGHT FOR TODAY

God is our sure hope, both for now and the future.

WISDOM FROM SCRIPTURE

As the deer pants for streams of water, so my soul pants for you, O God.

My soul thirsts for God, for the living God. When can I go and meet with God?

My tears have been my food day and night, while men say to me all day long, "Where is your God?"

These things I remember as I pour out my soul: how I used to go with the multitude, leading the procession to the house of God, with shouts of joy and thanksgiving among the festive throng.

Why are you downcast, O my soul? Why so disturbed within me? Put your hope in God, for I will yet praise him, my Savior and my God. My soul is downcast within me; therefore I will remember you from the land of the Jordan, the heights of Hermon—from Mount Mizar.

Deep calls to deep in the roar of your waterfalls; all your waves and breakers have swept over me.

By day the Lord directs his love, at night his song is with me—a prayer to the God of my life.

I say to God my Rock, "Why have you forgotten me? Why must I go about mourning, oppressed by the enemy?"

My bones suffer mortal agony as my foes taunt me, saying to me all day long, "Where is your God?"

Why are you downcast, O my soul? Why so disturbed within me? Put your hope in God, for I will yet praise him, my Savior and my God.

PSALM 42, NIV

INSIGHTS FROM DWIGHT L. MOODY

We are told to be ready to give a reason for the hope we have within us (see 1 Pt 3:15), and we need to find out what our hope is in. I believe there are people who are hoping when they have no grounds for hope. I don't know of any better way to find out whether we have a true reason for the hope within us than to look in Scripture to see what it has to say.

Faith is one thing and hope is another. When hope takes the place of faith, it is a snare. Faith is to work and trust. Someone has said that life is to enjoy and obey and be like God; but hope is to wait and trust—to wait and expect. In other words, hope is the daughter of faith. I heard a very godly man once say that joy was like the larks—they sang in the morning when it was light, but hope was like the nightingale that sang in the dark, so hope is really better than joy.

Most anyone can sing in the morning when everything is bright and going well. But hope sings in the dark, in the mist and the fog. It looks through all the mist and darkness into the clear day. Faith lays hold of what is in the Scripture; faith is laying hold of what is within the vale, and what is in heaven for us. We cannot get on any better without hope than we can without faith. The farmer who sows his seed, sows it in the hope of a harvest; the merchant buys his goods with the hope to find customers, and the student toils in the hope that he will reap later.

Hope in Scripture is never used to express a doubt. You cannot find Christians in the Bible who say they hope they are Christians. It is something that has already taken place. We don't hope we are Christians. If someone asks me if I am a married man, I would not say I hope I am. If someone asked me if I am an American, I would not say I hope I am. I was born in this country. So if I have been born of God, born of the Spirit—and I contend it is our privilege to know—I don't say, "I hope I am a Christian." I know in whom I have believed.

I will tell you what hope is used for in Scripture. It is used to express our hope of the resurrection or the coming of the Lord Jesus Christ—something to take place in the future. It is a sure hope. Almost every time the word *hope* is used in Scripture, it is used either to express our hope of the resurrection or the coming back of our Lord and Master. We are waiting for our Lord from heaven. We have not a doubt. It is a sure hope.

We ought to know we are His. We ought to know we have passed from death unto life. We ought to know in whom we have believed, that we are looking forward to the time when our bodies shall be raised incorruptible; when that which has been sown in weakness shall be raised in power. We are living in the glorious hope that when our dead shall come back again, the loved ones we laid away in cemeteries shall come back when the Lord of heaven descends with a shout. "For the Lord himself shall descend from heaven with a shout, with the voice of the archangel, and with the trump of God; and the dead in Christ shall rise first; then we who are alive and remain shall be caught up together with them in the clouds, to meet the Lord in the air; and so shall we ever be with the Lord" (1 Thes 4:16-17).

So we stand with our loins girded and our lights burning, waiting for the coming of the Master.

It says in Proverbs 11:23, "The desire of the righteous is only good, but the expectation of the wicked is wrath." And the psalmist said, "Happy is he that has the God of Jacob for his help, whose hope is in the Lord, his God" (146:5). It is not some resolution that he has made; it is not in some act of his; it is not that he has joined some church; it is not that he reads the Bible, or that he says his prayers. His expectation is from God; his hope is in God.

God will fulfill His Word. The trouble is, we are putting our hope in one another, and we are being disappointed. We are putting our hope in ourselves, and our treacherous hearts are disappointing us, and then we are cast down. We want to put our hope in Him, not ourselves. A well-grounded hope is good for all time.

Crowning Glory

QUESTIONS TO CONSIDER
1. What is your greatest hope in this life?
2. How can you tell whether this hope is based on God and His character?

A PRAYERFUL RESPONSE
Lord, I will put my hope in You, now and forever. Amen.

The Second Coming

Thought for Today
We are to watch for the second coming of Christ.

Wisdom From Scripture
[Jesus said,] "Heaven and earth will pass away, but my words will never pass away.

"No one knows about that day or hour, not even the angels in heaven, nor the Son, but only the Father.

"As it was in the days of Noah, so it will be at the coming of the Son of Man.

"For in the days before the flood, people were eating and drinking, marrying and giving in marriage, up to the day Noah entered the ark; and they knew nothing about what would happen until the flood came and took them all away. That is how it will be at the coming of the Son of Man.

"Two men will be in the field; one will be taken and the other left.

"Two women will be grinding with a hand mill; one will be taken and the other left.

"Therefore keep watch, because you do not know on what day your Lord will come.

"But understand this: If the owner of the house had known at what time of night the thief was coming, he would have kept watch and would not have let his house be broken into.

"So you also must be ready, because the Son of Man will come at an hour when you do not expect him."

MATTHEW 24:35-44, NIV

Insights From Dwight L. Moody

It is perfectly safe to take the Word of God just as we find it. If Christ tells us to watch, then watch! If He tells us to pray, then pray! If He tells us He will come again, wait for Him! Let the Church bow to the Word of God, rather than try to find out how these things can be. "Behold I come quickly," said Christ. "Even so come, Lord Jesus," should be the prayer of the Church.

Take the account of Christ's words at the communion table. It seems to me the devil has covered up the most precious thing about it. "For as often as ye eat this bread, and drink this cup, ye do show forth the Lord's death *till he come*" (1 Cor 11:26). But most people seem to think the Lord's table is the place for self-examination, repentance, and making good resolutions. Not at all; you spoil it that way. Communion is to remember the Lord's death, and we are to keep it up until He comes.

God, wake us up! And I know of no better way to do it than to get the Church looking for the return of the Lord.

Some people say, "Oh, you will discourage young converts if you preach that doctrine." That hasn't been my experience. Since I came to understand that my Lord is coming back again, I have felt like working three times as hard. I look on this world as a wrecked vessel. God gave me a lifeboat and said to me, "Moody, save all you can."

God will come in judgment to this world, but the children of God don't belong to this world; they are in it, not of it, like a ship in the water. This world is getting darker and darker; its ruin is coming nearer and nearer. If you have any unsaved friends on this wreck, you had better lose no time getting them off.

You might be thinking, "Do you then make the grace of God a failure?" No, grace is not a failure, but people are. They have been a failure everywhere when they have had their own way and been left to themselves. Christ will save His Church, but He will save His children by finally taking them out of the world. Don't take my word for it. Look this up in the Bible and receive it as the Word of God.

Matthew 24:50-51 says, "The lord of that servant shall come in a day when he looketh not for him, and in an hour that he is not aware of, and shall cut him asunder, and appoint him his portion with the hypocrites; there shall be weeping and gnashing of teeth." And 2 Peter 3:3-4 says, "Knowing this first, that there shall come in the last days scoffers, walking after their own lusts, and saying, Where is the promise of his coming? For since the fathers fell asleep, all things continue as they were from the beginning of the creation." Go out on the streets of this city, and ask people about the return of the Lord, and that is just what they would say, "Oh, yes; the Lord delays His coming!"

Yet Christ said to John, "Surely, I come quickly." And the last prayer in the Bible is, "Even so, come, Lord Jesus" (Rv 22:20).

The world waited for the first coming of the Lord, waited four thousand years, and then He came. He was here for thirty-three years and then He went away. But He left a promise that He would come again, and as the world watched and waited for His first coming, it did not watch in vain. So now, to them who wait for His appearing, shall He appear a second time unto salvation.

Now let the question be asked, "Am I ready to meet the Lord if He comes tonight?"

"Be ye ready, for in such an hour as ye think not the Son of Man cometh."

The Best of D.L. Moody

QUESTIONS TO CONSIDER
1. What does the second coming of Christ mean to you?
2. How can you live each day in light of the Lord's coming?

A PRAYERFUL RESPONSE
Lord, I am hoping and waiting for Your return. Amen.

DAY 39

A HOME IN HEAVEN

THOUGHT FOR TODAY
Christ has prepared a place for us in heaven.

WISDOM FROM SCRIPTURE
[Jesus said,] "Do not let your hearts be troubled. Trust in God; trust also in me.

"In my Father's house are many rooms; if it were not so, I would have told you. I am going there to prepare a place for you.

"And if I go and prepare a place for you, I will come back and take you to be with me that you also may be where I am.

"You know the way to the place where I am going."

Thomas said to him, "Lord, we don't know where you are going, so how can we know the way?"

Jesus answered, "I am the way and the truth and the life. No one comes to the Father except through me.

"If you really knew me, you would know my Father as well. From now on, you do know him and have seen him."

Philip said, "Lord, show us the Father and that will be enough for us."

Jesus answered: "Don't you know me, Philip, even after I have been among you such a long time? Anyone who has seen me has seen the Father. How can you say, 'Show us the Father'?

"Don't you believe that I am in the Father, and that the Father is in me? The words I say to you are not just my own. Rather, it is the Father, living in me, who is doing his work.

"Believe me when I say that I am in the Father and the Father is in me; or at least believe on the evidence of the miracles themselves.

"I tell you the truth, anyone who has faith in me will do what I have been doing. He will do even greater things than these, because I am going to the Father."

JOHN 14:1-12, NIV

INSIGHTS FROM DWIGHT L. MOODY

We have ample evidence in the Bible that there is such a place as heaven, and we have abundant manifestation that God's influence from heaven is felt among us. He is not in person among us, but only in spirit.

In 2 Chronicles 7:14 we read, "If my people, who are called by my name, shall humble themselves, and pray, and seek my face, and turn from their wicked ways, then will I hear from heaven, and will forgive their sin, and will heal their land." Here is a reference to heaven, and many might ask, "How far away is heaven? Can you tell us that?"

I don't know how far away it is, but there is one thing I can tell you. He can hear prayer as soon as the words are uttered. There has not been a prayer uttered that He has not heard; not a tear shed that He has not seen. What we want to know is that God is there, and Scripture tells us that. In 2 Chronicles 6:21 we read, "Hearken, therefore, unto the supplications of thy servant, and of thy people, Israel, which they shall make toward this place; hear thou from thy dwelling place, even from heaven; and when thou hearest, forgive."

It is clearly taught in the Word of God that the Father dwells in heaven. It is His dwelling place, and at the stoning of Stephen we see that Jesus is there, too. "But he [Stephen], being full of the Holy Spirit, looked up steadfastly into heaven, and saw the glory of God, and Jesus standing on the right hand of God" (Acts 7:55). With the eye of faith we can see Him there, too. By faith we shall be brought into His presence, and we shall be satisfied when we gaze upon Him.

We'll see Him by and by. It is not the jasper streets and golden gates that attract us to heaven. What are your palaces on earth—what is it that makes them so sweet? It is the presence of some loving wife or fond children. Let them be taken away and the charm of your home is gone. Christ is the charm of heaven. Yes, we shall see Him there. How sweet the thought that we shall dwell with Him forever and shall see the nails in His hands and in His feet, which He received for us.

I read about a mother in an eastern city who was stricken with consumption. At her dying hour she requested that her husband bring their children to her. The oldest one was brought first, and she laid her hand on his head and gave him her blessing and dying message. The next one was brought, and she gave him the same. One after another the children came to her bedside, until the infant was brought in. She took him and pressed him to her bosom, and the people in the room, fearing that she was straining her strength, took the child away from her. As this was done she turned to her husband and said, "I charge you, sir, bring all those children home with you."

And so God charges us. The promise is to ourselves and to our children. We can have our names written in heaven, and then, by the grace of God, we can call our children to us and know that their names are also recorded there. The great roll is being called, and those bearing the names are summoned every day, every hour. That great roll is being called now, and if your name were shouted, could you answer with joy?

A soldier fell in our war, and as he lay dying, he was heard to cry, "Here! Here."

Some of his comrades went to him, thinking he wanted water, but he said, "They are calling the roll of heaven, and I am answering." In a faint voice he whispered, "Here!" and passed away to heaven.

If that roll was called now, would you be ready to answer "Here"?

Let us wake up. There is work to do. Father and mothers, look to your children. If I could only speak to one group, I would preach to parents and try to show them the great responsibility that rests upon them—try to teach them how much more they should devote their lives to the secure and immortal treasure of heaven for their children than to spend their lives scraping together worldly goods for them.

Am I speaking to a prayerless father or mother? Settle the question of your own soul's salvation and pray for the son or daughter God has given to you.

New Sermons, Addresses, and Prayers of Dwight Lyman Moody

QUESTIONS TO CONSIDER
1. How do you know God has prepared a place for you in heaven?
2. Who do you look forward to meeting there?

A PRAYERFUL RESPONSE
Lord, thank You for preparing a place for me in heaven. Amen.

HEAVENLY TREASURES

THOUGHT FOR TODAY

Christ asks that we store up lasting treasures in heaven.

WISDOM FROM SCRIPTURE

[Jesus said,] "Do not store up for yourselves treasures on earth, where moth and rust destroy, and where thieves break in and steal.

"But store up for yourselves treasures in heaven, where moth and rust do not destroy, and where thieves do not break in and steal.

"For where your treasure is, there your heart will be also.

"The eye is the lamp of the body. If your eyes are good, your whole body will be full of light.

"But if your eyes are bad, your whole body will be full of darkness. If then the light within you is darkness, how great is that darkness!

"No one can serve two masters. Either he will hate the one and love the other, or he will be devoted to the one and despise the other. You cannot serve both God and Money.

"Therefore I tell you, do not worry about your life, what you will eat or drink; or about your body, what you will wear. Is not life more important than food, and the body more important than clothes?

"Look at the birds of the air; they do not sow or reap or store away in barns, and yet your heavenly Father feeds them. Are you not much more valuable than they?

"Who of you by worrying can add a single hour to his life?

"And why do you worry about clothes? See how the lilies of the field grow. They do not labor or spin.

"Yet I tell you that not even Solomon in all his splendor was dressed like one of these.

"If that is how God clothes the grass of the field, which is here today and tomorrow is thrown into the fire, will he not much more clothe you, O you of little faith?

"So do not worry, saying, 'What shall we eat?' or 'What shall we drink?' or 'What shall we wear?'

"For the pagans run after all these things, and your heavenly Father knows that you need them.

"But seek first his kingdom and his righteousness, and all these things will be given to you as well.

"Therefore do not worry about tomorrow, for tomorrow will worry about itself. Each day has enough trouble of its own."

MATTHEW 6:19-34, NIV

INSIGHTS FROM DWIGHT L. MOODY

If we are living as the Lord would have us live, our treasures are laid up in heaven, and not on the earth. I think we would be saved a great many painful hours, and a great deal of trouble, if we would just obey this portion of Scripture, and lay up our treasures in heaven. It is just as much a command to lay up our treasures in heaven, and not upon the earth, as it is a command not to steal.

It doesn't take long to tell where a person's treasure is. It doesn't take long to find out where a person's heart is. You talk with a person five minutes, and if he has his heart upon one object, you will find out. And if you want to find out

180

where a person's treasure is, it won't take long to find that out, either. The Bible tells us, "Where your treasure is, there shall your heart be also."

We have so many earthly minded people and so few people with heavenly minds because many have their whole hearts set upon earthly pleasures and objects, and few have their treasures laid up in heaven. If your treasure is here, you will be disappointed and in trouble and trial, when the Lord has told you plainly to lay up your treasures in heaven, where moth and rust do not corrupt, nor thieves break in and steal.

When you talk about heaven to the child of God, who has his treasure up yonder, you will see his heart is there. If a person's heart is in heaven, it's not an effort for him to talk about it. He cannot help it. And if our affections are set on things above and not on this earth, it will be easy for us to live for God. Now, here is the command: "Lay not up for yourselves treasures upon earth, ... but lay up for yourselves treasures in heaven."

Where is your treasure? In other words, where is your heart?

In Hebrews 11:13-14, we find these words: "These all died in faith, not having received the promises but having seen them afar off, and were persuaded of them, and embraced them, and confessed that they were strangers and pilgrims on the earth. For they that say such things declare plainly that they seek a country." Then in the tenth verse of the same chapter, speaking of Abraham, it says, "For he looked for a city which hath foundations, whose builder and maker is God." The moment Abraham caught sight of that city, he proclaimed himself a pilgrim and a stranger. The well-watered plains of Sodom had no temptation for him. He declared that he saw another country—a better country. He had turned his heart from this fleeting world, and Sodom with all its temptations didn't tempt him. He had something better. How poor a man is, no matter how much he has laid up in this world, if he has not his treasure laid up in heaven!

Many people are wondering why they don't grow in grace—why they don't have more spiritual power. The question is easily answered. They have their treasure down here. It is not necessary for a person to have money to have his treasure here. He may have his heart on pleasure; he may make an idol of his children, and that is the reason he is not growing in grace.

If we would only be wise and do as God tells us, we would mount up on wings, and would get nearer to heaven every day. We would get heavenly minded in our conversation and have less trouble than now. And so, my friends, let us just ask ourselves today: Where is our treasure? Is it on earth or in heaven? What are we doing? What is the aim of our lives? Are we just living to accumulate money, or to get a position in the world for our children? Or are we trying to secure those treasures we can safely lay up in heaven, becoming rich toward God?

I have known men who have been up in balloons, and they have told me that when they want to rise higher, they just throw out some of the sand with which they ballast the balloon. I believe one reason so many people are earthly minded and have so little of the spirit of heaven is that they have too much ballast in the shape of love for earthly joys and gains. Throw out some of the sand, and you will rise higher.

I heard of a man who said he did not know what to do with his money. It was a burden to him to take care of it. I could not help but think of what I would tell him to do with it. I could tell him where to invest it, where it would bring an eternal profit.

I hope to live to see the day when people will be as anxious to make investments for the Lord as for themselves, and then people won't be putting as much money in railroad shares, and so much in bank stocks, or so much in a mine in the mountain. They will put it in good security, where it will draw returns for the Lord. That is the investment I think we ought to live for.

Dwight L. Moody

QUESTIONS TO CONSIDER
1. What do you treasure the most in life?
2. Specifically, how can you store up treasures in heaven?

A PRAYERFUL RESPONSE
Lord, I will store up treasures in heaven. But most of all, I will treasure You. Amen.

BOOKS OF DWIGHT L. MOODY'S SERMONS

The books that contain D.L. Moody's sermons are too numerous to list here. However, these are the works the compiler consulted for creating *Only Trust Him*.

Addresses of D.L. Moody
Crowning Glory
Dwight L. Moody
Dwight Lyman Moody's Life Work and Gospel Sermons
Evenings with Moody and Sankey
Fifty Sermons and Evangelistic Talks
Glad Tidings
Great Joy
Moody: His Words, Work, and Workers
Moody's Great Sermons
Moody's Latest Sermons
New Sermons, Addresses, and Prayers of Dwight Lyman Moody
Sowing and Reaping
The Best of D.L. Moody
The Home Work of D.L. Moody
The Overcoming Life
"Thou Fool!"
"To All People"
"To the Work! To the Work!"
The Gospel Awakening
Twelve Select Sermons
Wondrous Love

ABOUT THE COMPILER

With the *Life Messages of Great Christians* series, Judith Couchman hopes you'll be encouraged and enlightened by people who have shared their spiritual journeys through the printed word.

Judith owns Judith & Company, a writing and editorial consulting business. She has also served as the creator and founding editor-in-chief of *Clarity* magazine, managing editor of *Christian Life,* editor of *Sunday Digest,* director of communications for The Navigators, and director of new product development for NavPress.

Besides speaking to women's and professional conferences, Judith is the author or compiler of twenty books and many magazine articles. In addition, she has received awards for her work in secondary education, religious publishing, and corporate communications.

She lives in Colorado.